Reading for the Citizen of the World
世界公民读本（文库）

FOUNDATIONS of DEMOCRACY

Reading for the Citizen of the World
世界公民读本（文库）

Foundations of Democracy

民主的基础丛书

主编 赵文彤

Privacy
隐私

〔美〕Center for Civic Education (公民教育中心) 著

刘小小 译

隐私
PRIVACY

责任
RESPONSIBILITY

正义
JUSTICE

权威
AUTHORITY

金城出版社
GOLD WALL PRESS

FOUNDATIONS of DEMOCRACY

AUTHORITY PRIVACY RESPONSIBILITY JUSTICE

English Edition Copyright ©2009. Center for Civic Education. Calabasas, CA, USA.

著作权合同登记图字：B11002795-01-2011-3502

图书在版编目(CIP)数据

隐私 /（美国）公民教育中心著；刘小小译. —北京
：金城出版社，2011.6
　（世界公民读本文库/赵文彤主编）
　书名原文：Privacy
　ISBN 978-7-80251-928-2

　Ⅰ. ①隐… Ⅱ. ①美… ②刘… Ⅲ. ①隐私权-青年
读物②隐私权-少年读物 Ⅳ. ①D913-49

中国版本图书馆CIP数据核字（2011）第075248号

隐私

作　　者	CENTER FOR CIVIC EDUCATION (美国)公民教育中心
责任编辑	袁东旭
开　　本	710毫米×1000毫米 1/16
印　　张	16
字　　数	245千字
版　　次	2011年8月第1版 2011年8月第1次印刷
印　　刷	北京联兴华印刷厂
书　　号	ISBN 978-7-80251-928-2
定　　价	35.00元

出版发行	金城出版社 北京市朝阳区和平街11区37号楼 邮编：100013
发 行 部	(010)84254364
编 辑 部	(010)64210080
总 编 室	(010)64228516
网　　址	http://www.jccb.com.cn
电子邮箱	jinchengchuban@163.com
法律顾问	陈鹰律师事务所　(010)64970501

本书承蒙郭昌明基金资助印行

该基金以一位年近百岁的母亲的名字命名，她和中国近百年来一代又一代的普通母亲一样，将自己对人生和世界最美好的希望全部寄托给了成长中的中国式的世界公民。

The mission of the Center for Civic Education is to promote an enlightened, competent, and responsible citizenry. The curriculum materials prepared under this mandate are designed to advance this outcome. It is our goal to share these materials as widely as possible, to make them available to the students, teachers, and parents of the world, and not to limit distribution or to make profits for any individual.

美国公民教育中心以提高全体公民的文明程度、能力素养和责任感为己任，据此编写的课程教材，为达到这一结果而设计。我们的目标是尽可能广泛地分享这些课程教材，让世界上的学生、教师和家长都可以受用，不受限制地分发，也不为任何个人谋取利益。

CENTER FOR CIVIC EDUCATION

5145 Douglas Fir Road
Calabasas, CA 91302 - USA
818.591.9321 - Fax 818.591.9330
cce@civiced.org
www.civiced.org

人类命运与责任共同体时代呼唤世界公民
——世界公民读本（文库）出版说明

刘建华

引子

　　早在大约 250 年前，中国与世界公民 (The Citizen of the World) 这个英文词组，就有过一次美丽的的邂逅。18 世纪 60 年代，中国在西方的许多思想家那里，被理想化为一个美好而神秘的国度，哥德斯密 (Oliver Goldsmith，1728—1774) 就是在这样的时代背景下，以"中国人的信札"(Chinese Letters) 为名，发表连载文章，借此讥讽英国的社会弊病，两年后（1763）结集出版，题名为：The Citizen of the World or Letters of a Chinese Philosopher living in London to his Friends in the East. 翻译成中文，是《世界公民—— 一位旅居伦敦的中国哲学家写给他的东方朋友的信札》。

　　此后过了约 150 年，大约距今 100 年前的 1914 年，一个在美国的中国人应验了歌德斯密的这个噱头式的玩笑。根据邵建先生发表在《大学人文》（广西师范大学出版社 2008 年 5 月版）的文章，这一年，在美国康奈尔大学的学生宿舍里，胡适在自己的一篇日记中，以《大同主义之先哲名言》为题，抄录了以下数则关于"世界公民"的先哲名言，这些名言以无言的方式，影响了无数个"胡适"们，并通过他们在后来的一个世纪里影响了无数中国人——

亚里斯提卜说过，智者的祖国就是世界。
——第欧根尼·拉尔修：《亚里斯提卜》第十三章

当有人问及他是何国之人时，第欧根尼回答道：
"我是世界之公民。"
——第欧根尼·拉尔修：《亚里斯提卜》第十三章

苏格拉底说，他既不是一个雅典人，也不是一个希腊人，
只不过是一个世界公民。
——普卢塔：《流放论》

我的祖国是世界，我的宗教是行善。
——T. 潘恩：《人类的权利》第五章

世界是我的祖国，人类是我的同胞。
——W.L. 加里森：《解放者简介》

一

进入 21 世纪以来，全球气候变暖的危机日益明显，与此相关的多种全球性危机日益增多，人类仿佛在一夜之间变得比以往任何时代都更加亲如兄弟、情同手足，地球比以往任何时候都更像是一个风雨飘摇中的小小的村落。这不只是全球经济一体化和信息技术与交通高度发达的结果，也不只是人类追求世界大同理想社会的结果，而是任何一个国家和民族都无法单独应对的全球共同的危机，让我们人类不得不彼此靠近，不能不唇齿相依，除了学会成为彼此一家的世界公民，学会互相之间兄弟姐妹般的友善和宽容，我们已经别无选择。

二

我们因此正在走向"人类命运共同体和全球责任共同体"的特殊时代，世界各国人民因此必须走出宗教文化壁垒，跨越意识形态障碍，超越政治制度边界，以世界公民的身份，与其他国家和民族的人民一道，共同承担起人类社会的可持续发展责任。我们每一个人不仅需要具有自觉的世界公民责任意识，更需要具有能承担起世界公民责任的基本素质和技能——在这样一个事关我们每一个人现在的生存质量、决定我们每一个家庭明天的

生活希望的全球性危机时代，我们每一个人都不能不从头开始，学会以世界公民的方式生存。

三

我们因此需要一个全球普遍适用的世界公民教育体系，但我们又身处多元格局的差异化社会之中，我们因此永远不可能有一部放之四海而皆准的世界公民统编教材，但是我们却可以而且必须互相参考和借鉴。我们因此倡导"互相阅读"和"比较阅读"式的世界公民教育，这本身就是一种承担共同责任的世界公民行为，是人类面对全球性危机时，首先需要的一种协商、协调、协同的智慧和行为。我们相信，尽管一方面，世界各国发展不平衡，世界各民族和地区的文化各不相同，应对全球性危机和承担世界公民责任的方式、方法和路径各不相同，但是，另一方面，世界各国无论贫富，世界各地无论远近，世界各民族文化无论有多么地不同，都毫无例外地、没有差别地、不可逃避地承受着同样的全球性危机的影响和压力，都必须协调一致，在人类的共同拯救行动中才能最终拯救自己。

四

综观世界各国的公民教育，无论是发达国家还是发展中国家，基本素质和基本技能都是公民教育的核心内容，唯其如此，世界各国的公民教育经验才具有互相参考和借鉴的可能性，不同语言的公民教育读本才具有互相阅读的必要性。

在众多国家出版的众多公民教育读本中，美国公民教育中心的一整套教材，在这方面最具有代表性。这套公民教育读本，可以说是"最高地位的社会名流邀请最高学问的专家一道，弯下腰来，以最低的姿态，奉献给他们认为是最高大的幼儿、少年、青年们的《公民圣经》"。这套由美国以及世界上多个国家多方面领域的专家经过多年精心编修的读本，没有高深的理论，没有刻板的道理，没有号称伟大的思想体系，没有不可置疑的绝对真理，而是结合人生成长的不同阶段，针对不同年龄青少年的学习、生活和成长实际，引导学生，通过自己的独立判断、反思鉴别、团队合作、谈判妥协、陈述坚持、提案答辩等理性的方法和智慧的工具，在观察、发现、认知、处理身边各种与公民权利和责任有关的问题的过程中，成长为一个具有公民美德基本素质和履行社会责任的基本技能的合格公民。

五

我们深知，无论多么好的公民素质和技能，离开了养成这种素质和技能的国度，就不一定有效，我们因此只是将这套美国公民教育读本作为中国公民的参考读物，原原本本地译介过来，用作借鉴，而非直接用作教材；我们深知，无论多么好的公民教育读本，离开了产生这种读本的文字语言环境，就很难领略其中丰富的意蕴，我们因此采用中英文对照的方式出版，即便是当作学习美国英语的泛读教材，也不失为一种明智的选择，因为这套读本用最基本的词汇和最浅显的文体，最准确地阐释了美国最基本的社会实质和美国公民最基本的生活真实。

六

《世界公民读本》（文库），是一项长期性的、庞大的公益出版计划，其宗旨在于倡导全社会的"公民阅读"。 公民阅读和私人兴趣阅读不一样的地方在于，私人阅读更关注个体自身的心灵世界、个人的知识需求和个性化的审美愉悦，而公民阅读更关心的是公共生活的领域、人类共同的价值和世界更好的未来。从这个意义上来说，公民阅读是一种更加需要精神品德和高尚情怀的开放式阅读、互动式阅读和参与式阅读，也正是在这个意义上，可以说，我们翻译出版给国人阅读的这套《世界公民读本》，其实也是真正意义上的《好人读本》、《成功读本》、《领袖读本》，是每一个人，要想成长、成熟、成功的基本教科书，是任何人一生中的"第一启蒙读本"。

七

我们的民族是一个崇尚"好人"的民族，深受"穷则独善其身，达则兼济天下"的自我完善文化影响，更有所谓"不在其位、不谋其政"的古老训条，这些都很容易被借用来为我们远离社会理想、逃避公民责任构建自我安慰的巢穴。人们因此更愿意以"独善"的"好人"自居，而怯于以"兼济"的"好公民"自励。

尽管我们的传统是一个没有公民的好人社会传统，但我们的时代却是一个需要好公民的大社会时代，在这样的文化纠结中，就让我们用世界公民的阅读方式延续中国的好人传统，用好人的传统善意理解当今的公民世界。这可以说是我们编辑出版《世界公民读本》（文库）的初衷。

八

我们期待着有一天，公民这个称呼，能够像"贤人"一样，成为令每一个中国人都值得骄傲的赞许；世界公民这个身份，能够像"圣人"一样，成为中华传统至高无上的美德的代名词。

我们相信有一天，一个普通的中国人面对世界的时候，也能够像美国的奥巴马一样，以世界公民的身份向世界的公民们说：

"Tonight, I speak to you not as a candidate for President, but as a citizen— a proud citizen of the United States, and a fellow citizen of the world. "（今晚，我并不是以一个总统候选人的身份在这里向大家演讲，而是以一位公民—— 一位以美国为荣的公民和一位世界公民的身份跟大家讲话。）

"I am a citizen of the world." 我是一个世界公民。你准备好了吗？

编者语

　　这是一些将民主与法治当作信仰，相信它能够成为社会的秩序原则与社会运行方式，并坚信理性力量的知识精英，历经数年共同精心编纂的一部书。他们满怀激情、充满智慧，以建筑一座理想中恢宏大厦的决心，做着构建最扎实地基的工作——公民教育。

　　被命名为《民主的基础》的这一辑的读者对象，是甫将开始独立社会生活的青年。这些青年，正是保证前人着力思考过、倾心建设过的民主与法治机制——同时也是具有普世价值的文化传统和社会生活信念，能够得以延续的基石。

　　作为美国高中的课程读本，《民主的基础》由《权威》、《隐私》、《责任》、《正义》四个部分构成。所涉问题常常会触碰到个体的自我面对群体的他者时的一些核心价值冲突，令我们本能、直觉的感受纠结与困扰。但是，我们都知道，这世界是由一个个独立的个体组成的一个共同体，社会共有的秩序与幸福是达成个体幸福的基础。在纷繁复杂的人际社会中、在相互冲突的利益与价值面前，必须权衡利弊，做出理性的思考与选择。因此，只有当一个社会有更多能够独立思考的人、以社会的共同利益为目标捍卫个人权利的人，我们才能够期待这个社会更加和谐美好。

　　该丛书的要旨不仅是带领研习者广泛而深入的思考权威、隐私、责任、正义这些至关重要的问题，更是通过思想智慧、知识经验给出了一个叫做"知识工具"的东西。"它是一种思想工具，是研究问题和制定决策的一系列思路与方法的集合。"运用这些工具，不仅能帮助我们更好地解析这些核心理念，更通过由理念到操作层面的分析与权衡，令研读者通过熟练运用具体的指标体系，形成对研究对象的判断与决策，在面对多重利益交叠的复杂的社会政治生活、决定我们的态度和行动方式的时候，超越情感，不是凭主观感受，而是理性、平和、有序的使用知识工具做出衡量与选择。

　　可以说，这套书是一部精粹的法治文化及公民教育领域的思想方法读本，是了解美国核心民主法治建构理念与公平公正处世方略的钥匙，是把握理性权衡与处置个体与社会共同体之间利益与冲突的工具，同时也是学习最简洁、规范、实用的文化英语和法律英语的范本。相信该丛书会从多个方面给予我们启迪。

Foundations of Democracy introduces you to four ideas which are basic to our constitutional form of government: authority, privacy, responsibility, and justice. These are not only ideas that need to be grasped in order to understand the foundations of our government, but they are crucial to evaluating the important differences between a constitutional democracy and a society that is not free.

《民主的基础》将向你们介绍美国政府的宪政模式中的四种基本观念：权威、隐私、责任和正义。理解和掌握这四种观念，不仅有助于理解美国政府的立国之本，更是评估和区分"宪政民主"与"不自由的社会"的关键。

Preface

Foundations of Democracy introduces you to four ideas which are basic to our constitutional form of government: authority, privacy, responsibility, and justice. These are not only ideas that need to be grasped in order to understand the foundations of our government, but they are crucial to evaluating the important differences between a constitutional democracy and a society that is not free.

There are costs or burdens that we must bear in order to preserve our freedom and the values on which our nation was founded. There are many situations in which hard choices need to be made between competing values and interests. In this course of study, you will be challenged to discuss and debate situations involving the use of authority and the protection of privacy. You will be asked to decide how responsibilities should be fulfilled and how justice could be achieved in a number of situations.

You will learn different approaches and ideas, which we call "intellectual tools," to evaluate these situations. Intellectual tools help you think clearly about issues of authority, privacy, responsibility, and justice. They help you develop your own positions, and support your positions which reasons.

The knowledge and skills you gain in this course of study will assist you not only in addressing issues of public policy, but also in everyday situations you face in your private life. By thinking for yourself, reaching your own conclusions, and defending your positions, you can be a more effective and active citizen in a free society.

前　言

　　《民主的基础》将向你们介绍美国政府的宪政模式中的四种基本观念：权威、隐私、责任和正义。理解和掌握这四种观念，不仅有助于理解美国政府的立国之本，更是评估和区分"宪政民主"与"不自由的社会"的关键。

　　为了维护我们的国家得以建立的自由和价值，我们必须付出代价或承担责任，我们也必须在许多相互冲突的价值和利益中做出选择。在本课程的学习中，你们将会针对运用权威和保护隐私的案例进行讨论和辩论，你们将要回答在一系列情况下应当如何承担责任、怎样才能实现正义的问题。

　　在本课程中，你们将学到各种不同的方法和观念（在这里我们统称为"知识工具"），并运用这些工具来评估不同的案例和情况。知识工具不仅将帮助你们对有关权威、隐私、责任和正义的问题进行更清晰的思考，也将有助于你们形成自己的观点，并通过推理来论证自己的观点。

　　在本课程学习过程中所获得的知识与技能，不仅将有助于你们应对未来的公共政策问题，也能帮助你们面对个人生活中的日常情况。通过独立思考，形成自己的观点并对此进行论证。作为一个公民的你，将更有效、更主动地投身于自由的社会中。

PRIVACY
Table of Contents

目录

 宪法和最高法院如何保护了隐私权？

How have the Constitution and the Supreme Court protected the right to privacy?

Introduction

"The right of the people to be secure in their persons, houses, papers, and effects, against unreasonable searches and seizures, shall not be violated ...."

The Fourth Amendment to the United States Constitution, quoted above, requires the government to respect our right to privacy. Today, the right to privacy includes much more than the protection of our homes and persons against unreasonable searches and seizures. The Supreme Court has recognized that privacy also involves being able to decide for ourselves what personal information we will share with others and how we will resolve certain issues that fundamentally affect our lives, such as whether we will marry or have children.

Although the Bill of Rights does not specifically refer to a right to privacy, the Supreme Court has found protections of privacy in the Fourth Amendment, in the Fifth Amendment's privilege against self-incrimination, in the Third Amendment's prohibition against housing soldiers in private homes, and in the First Amendment's protection of assembly and expression. Most importantly, the court has determined that the right to privacy is a fundamental part of the "liberty" guaranteed by the Fourteenth Amendment.

The right to privacy is an essential protection of human freedom and dignity. Privacy is valuable not only for itself, but also for the enjoyment of our rights to property and to freedom of thought, expression, religion, and conscience. Without the right to privacy, these other important rights would not mean very much at all.

But the right to privacy is not absolute; there are times when an individual's right to privacy must be limited to protect society's need for order and information. As Americans, we need to be able to think and decide for ourselves when it is reasonable to limit our right to privacy to protect other important interests of our society.

导言

　　"人民的人身、住宅、文件和财产有不受无理搜查和扣押的权利，不得侵犯。"

　　以上美国宪法第四修正案的条款要求政府尊重我们的隐私权。今天我们的隐私权除了保护我们的住宅和人身免受无理的搜查和扣押之外，还包含了更多内容。最高法院承认，隐私包括人们能够自愿与他人分享的个人信息，以及人们会如何处理某些对自己生活产生重要影响的问题，例如：我们是否要结婚或者是否要生养孩子。

　　尽管《权利法案》中并没有特别提到隐私权，但最高法院在第四修正案中找到了保护隐私的条款；在第五修正案中反对自证其罪的特权（译者注：自证其罪指刑事案件中的作不利于自己或有可能使自己受到刑事起诉的证言，美国宪法认定此种证言不能作为合法证据）；在第三修正案中规定士兵不得在民用房屋中驻扎；在第一修正案中保护了集会和言论自由。最重要的是，通过第十四修正案的认可，法院判定隐私权是"自由"的一个重要组成部分。

　　隐私权是对人类自由和尊严的基本保障。隐私的价值不仅在于它本身，同时它对我们享有财产权，以及享有思想、言论、宗教和良知的自由都同样重要。没有隐私权，其他这些重要的权利对我们来说也就失去了意义。

　　但是，隐私权并不是一种绝对的权利；有时候为了保障社会对秩序和信息的需要，必须限制个人的隐私权。作为美国公民，我们需要能够独立思考并决定，为了保护我们社会中的其他重要利益，在什么时候需要合理限制隐私权。

This study of privacy should help you gain a greater understanding of its importance. It should also help you deal more effectively with issues of privacy as they arise in your daily life as an individual in a free society.

　　本课有关隐私的学习将能帮助你们更好地理解隐私的重要性，同时也将帮助身为自由社会个体的你们，更有效地处理日常生活中的个人隐私问题。

Unit One

What Is the Importance of Privacy?

Purpose of Unit

This unit will help you develop a greater understanding of the meaning and importance of privacy. You will learn to identify and describe examples of privacy in a variety of situations and to discriminate between situations in which privacy does and does not exist.

You also will learn some common ways people behave to protect their privacy, and you will examine the privacy needs of individuals and institutions.

第一单元：隐私的重要性是什么？

单元目标

本单元将有助于你们更全面地理解隐私的含义及其重要性。你们将会学习在各种不同情况下找出并描述隐私的案例，并学会区别确实存在隐私或没有隐私的不同情况。

你们也将学会人们通常用来保护自己隐私的方法，同时研究个人和公共机构对隐私的需求。

 How do these photographs illustrate the importance of privacy?

这些照片如何体现出隐私的重要性？

LESSON 1
What Is Privacy?

> ### Purpose of Lesson
>
> This lesson introduces you to the importance of privacy and defines privacy as it is used in this textbook. When you have completed this lesson, you should be able to distinguish between situations in which privacy does and does not exist. You also should be able to describe common objects of privacy and the reasons people may wish to have privacy in specific situations.

Terms to Know

Privacy   solitude   objects of privacy

Critical Thinking Exercise

EXAMINING DEGREES OF PRIVACY

Most people will share some information about themselves with just about anyone, but keep other information to themselves or only share it with close friends or family. Similarly, people do not mind doing some things in public, while they will do other things only in private or with people they know and trust.

In this exercise, create separate lists of the kinds of information and activities that you think people would

• be willing to share with strangers, such as newspaper or TV reporters, librarians, or government census workers

• be willing to share with classmates, neighbors, and other acquaintances

• be willing to share only with certain close friends or relatives

• not be willing to share with anyone

第一课：隐私是什么?

本课目标

本课将向你们介绍隐私的重要性，并定义本课中所使用的"隐私"。学完本课后，你们应当能够区分确实存在隐私和没有隐私的不同情况。你们也应当能够描述隐私的一般内容，以及在某些特定情况下人们希望保有隐私的原因。

掌握词汇

隐私　　　　孤独　　　　　　隐私的对象

重点思考练习

研究隐私的程度

大多数人愿意与任何人分享某些关于自己的信息，但有些信息则需要保密或只与最亲密的朋友或家人分享。同样地，人们并不介意在公开场合做某些事，但有些事他们只会在私密的场合或与自己了解和信任的人在一起时才会做。

在本次练习中，分别列出以下各种你们认为人们会：

- 愿意与陌生人分享的信息和活动，例如报纸或电视台记者、图书馆管理员或政府人口普查工作人员
- 愿意与同班同学、邻居和其他熟人分享的信息和活动
- 只愿意与某些亲密的朋友或亲人分享的信息和活动
- 不愿意与任何人分享的信息和活动

Each list should include four or five items. Work with a study partner or in small groups to create the lists. After everyone has finished, each pair or group of students should share their lists with the class. As a class, discuss the following questions:

1.What are the similarities among the lists?

2.What are the common characteristics of the information and activities people keep most private?

3.How would you feel if the information and activities you keep most private were broadcast on the TV news?

4.How would you feel if you could not share private information with your closest friends or relatives? How would it affect your relationships with them?

 What information about yourself are you willing to share with your classmates or a close friend? What information are you not willing to share at all? ☞

以上列出的每种信息和和活动中应当包括 4 或 5 件事。与一位同学一起或分小组集体讨论列出清单。然后，每一对或每一组同学应当与全班分享自己列出的清单。全班一起讨论以下问题：

1.　每组同学列出的清单之间有什么相同之处？

2.　人们最私密的信息和活动有什么共同特征？

3.　如果你最希望保密的信息和活动被新闻媒体曝光了，你会有什么感觉？

4.　如果你无法与你最亲密的朋友或亲人分享私人信息，你会有什么感觉？这将怎样影响你和他们之间的关系？

你愿意与你的同学或亲密的朋友分享哪些个人信息？哪些是你完全不想与任何人分享的？父母？同学？日记？

What is privacy?

As you have seen, privacy involves the ability to control or decide the extent to which information will be shared with others. But privacy also involves other things. For our purposes, privacy can be defined as the right to be left alone. This right can be threatened or invaded in different ways. We say "leave me alone" when someone asks us questions we do not want to answer; we also say "leave me alone" when we want someone to go away, or when someone is bothering us or interfering with something we are doing. Thus, the right to privacy may include:

• the right to decide whether information will be shared with others

• the right to solitude-that is, to be alone, away from other people

• the right to be free from the interference of others

The things we want to keep others from finding out about, observing, or interfering with are called **objects of privacy**. Objects of privacy may include:

• **facts** such as your birthplace, who your parents are, and your age or weight

• **actions** such as where you go or who you see

• **places and possessions** such as your room or the contents of a box or closet

• **thoughts and feelings** such as who you like and dislike, what you are afraid of, and what your religious or political beliefs are

• **communications** such as your letters or telephone conversations

Critical Thinking Exercise

EXAMINING SITUATIONS THAT INVOLVE PRIVACY

Read the following situations. List the numbers that are examples of privacy. Then answer the 'What do you think?" questions. Be prepared to share your answers with the class.

1. Tomas went into his room to talk with his friend Roberto because he did not want his mother to hear them.

2. Sometimes Farid went to the park to draw pictures so his family would not tease him about his drawings.

3. Misha walked up to Steven and said, "The basketball tournament starts today."

隐私是什么？

正如你们所看到的，隐私涉及到控制或决定与他人分享信息的程度的能力。但隐私也包括其他事情，在本课中，隐私可以被定义为"独处的权利"，这一权利可能会受到不同方式的威胁或侵犯。当人们问到我们并不想回答的某些问题时，我们会说"让我一个人待一会儿"；当我们希望他人走开或当有人打扰或干涉我们正在做的事情时，我们也会说"让我一个人待一会儿"。因此，隐私权可能包括以下方面：

- 决定是否要与他人分享信息的权利
- 独处的权利，即远离他人、独自一人
- 不受他人干扰的权利

我们不想让他人发现、看到或干涉的事情被称为隐私的内容。隐私的内容可能包括：

- 一些事实，例如：你的出生地、你的父母是谁、你的年龄和体重等
- 一些行为，例如：你要去哪里、你要见谁等
- 地点和财产，例如：你的房间、你的盒子或橱柜里的东西
- 思想和感受，例如：你喜欢谁、你讨厌谁、你害怕什么、你的宗教或政治信仰等
- 通讯，例如：你的信件或电话交谈内容等

重点思考练习

研究涉及到隐私的情境

阅读以下情境案例，选出当中包含隐私的案例，回答"你怎么看？"这一部分的问题，准备好与全班分享你的答案。

1. 托马斯走进自己的房间与朋友罗伯特说话，因为他不想让他的妈妈听到。
2. 有时法里德会去公园画画，这样他的家人就不会取笑他的画。
3. 米莎走上前对史蒂文说："篮球赛今天开始。"

4.Jessie and Loretta were best friends. They had a place in the mall where they met on Saturdays, but they agreed not to let anyone else know where it was.

5.Tonya went for a walk in the forest and suddenly realized she was lost. Tonya yelled for help, but no one could hear her. Now she was really alone.

6.When Alita got her report card,she kept it secret from her friends.

7.Although Theo supported the proposal to send troops overseas to restore order, he did not speak about it to his friends at work because they were opposed to the idea.

What do you think?

Answer the following questions for each situation that is an example of privacy.

1.Why is this situation an example of privacy?

2.Who wants to keep something private?

3.What is the object of privacy?

4.From whom is something to be kept private?

5.Why do you suppose the person wanted privacy?

Using the Lesson

1. Write several rules that you would like people to obey to protect your privacy at school. Be prepared to explain your rules to the class.

2. Bring a news clipping to class or report on a TV news program that illustrates an issue involving privacy. Be prepared to explain the issue to your class.

3. While you are studying privacy, keep a privacy notebook or journal. Over the next twenty-four hours, note at least five situations involving privacy, and answer the following questions about the situations:

• Who wishes to keep something private?

• What is the object of privacy?

• From whom does the person want to keep the object private?

Then explain why the person might have wanted to keep the object private.

4. 杰西和洛雷塔是最好的朋友，她们每周六都在购物中心里的某个地方碰面，但她们约定不让任何人知道这个地方。

5. 汤亚到森林里散步。突然，她意识到自己迷路了，于是她大声地呼救，却没人能听见。现在她真的是孤立无援了。

6. 阿尔塔收到自己的成绩单后把它藏了起来，不想让她的朋友们看到。

7. 虽然西奥支持向海外派兵、恢复当地秩序的提议，但他并没有在办公室里跟他的同事们提起这件事，因为他们都反对这个提议。

你怎么看?

针对以上每个情境中包含了隐私的案例，回答以下问题：

1. 为什么这个案例与隐私有关？
2. 谁希望将某些事情保密？
3. 隐私的内容是什么？
4. 这些事情要对哪些人保密？
5. 你认为案例中的这个人为什么需要保护隐私？

知识运用

1. 在学校，为了保护你的隐私，列出几项你希望大家遵守的规则，并准备向全班同学说明你的规则。

2. 找一篇有关隐私的新闻剪报，或一个关于隐私的电视新闻节目，准备与全班解释说明其中涉及的隐私问题。

3. 在学习隐私部分时，写一本有关隐私的笔记或日记。在接下来的 24 小时里，记下至少五个涉及隐私的情况，并针对每种情况回答以下问题：

   · 谁希望将某些事情保密？

   · 隐私的对象是什么？

   · 这些事情要对哪些人保密？

   然后解释你所列举的案例中的这个人为什么想要保密。

LESSON 2
How Do People Maintain Their Privacy?

Purpose of Lesson

This lesson describes different ways people behave to maintain their privacy. When you have finished this lesson, you should be able to explain some common ways people behave to keep others from observing or finding out about objects of privacy.

Terms to Know

isolation

secrecy

confidentiality

exclusion

How do people behave to keep things private?

The following are some of the most common ways that people behave to protect their privacy:

1.Isolation. People may isolate themselves, that is, they may keep away from other people. For example, they may stay in a room or a house or go to some far-away place to live.

2.Secrecy. People may keep objects of privacy secret, that is, they may purposely not tell others about them. For example, you and your friends may keep your plans for a weekend a secret, or agree not to tell anyone about something you have seen or done. People may keep facts about their income or their debts a secret.

3.Confidentiality. When people share private information with someone who is expected and trusted not to tell anyone else, this is called confidentiality. For example, you may tell a secret to a friend, relative, or guidance counselor and expect him or her notto repeat the information. What people say in private to their doctors, lawyers, and religious counselors is confidential.

第二课：人们如何保护自己的隐私？

本课目标

本课描述了人们保护隐私的不同方式。学完本课后，你们应当能够说明某些人们用来避免他人注意和发现自己隐私的常用方式。

掌握词汇

隔离

保密

私密

排斥

人们如何保护某些隐私？

以下是人们用行动来保护自己隐私的某些最常见的方式：

1. **隔离**：人们可以把自己隔离起来，也就是说，他们可以让自己远离他人。例如，他们会待在房间里或屋子里，或者到某些偏远的地方居住。

2. **保密**：人们可能会对某些私人的事情保密，也就是说，他们会故意不告诉别人这些秘密。例如，你和你的朋友们把你们的周末计划当做秘密，或者约好不告诉任何人你们看到或做过的事情。人们可能会对自己的收入或债务保密。

3. **私密**：当人们将私人信息与自己尊重和信任的人分享，并相信这个人不会告诉其他人的时候，就叫"私密"。例如，你可能会将一个秘密告诉一个朋友、亲人或心理辅导老师，并希望他或她不会把这件事传出去。人们对自己的医生、律师和神职人员私下里说的话都是私密的。

4.Exclusion. People may keep things private or secret by excluding others. For example, you may keep something private by not allowing others to look into your wallet, locker, room, or home. Some government agencies try to maintain secrecy by not allowing unauthorized people to go into certain buildings or on the grounds of military bases.

Critical Thinking Exercise

IDENTIFYING HOW PEOPLE MAINTAIN PRIVACY

As you read the following selection adapted from the book, Assignment: Rescue by Varian Fry, identify the different ways people behave to keep things private. Then answer the "What do you think?" questions. Be prepared to discuss your answers with the class.

Excerpt from Assignment: Rescue

Hitler's rise to power in Germany in the late 1930s began a time of terror for millions of Jews and others on the Nazi's hit list. Many fled Germany's borders to the unoccupied zone of southern France. But when France fell to Hitler in June of 1940, these refugees were in danger of being turned over to the Gestapo, who imprisoned, tortured, and executed them in concentration camps.

A group of New Yorkers shocked by the Third Reich's actions formed the Emergency Rescue Committee. Their goal was to get artists, writers, musicians, scientists, professors, and political figures out of France before the Gestapo seized them. They had to find the right person to be their agent, someone who would be allowed into France and be willing to risk the dangers of a secret mission. Thus, Varian Fry-a man with no secret agent experience but who had an excellent cover through the International Y.M.C.A.-managed to smuggle more than a thousand refugees out of Marseilles in thirteen months through his efficient underground organization.

With my three helpers-Beamish the outside man, Franzi the interviewer, and Lena the secretary-we interviewed those who came to seek our help all day long. We wrote their names down on white file cards, but we never listed their addresses. In case of a sudden raid by the police, we did not want a lot of cards lying around with addresses where people could be picked up and arrested.

4. 排斥：人们可能会通过排斥他人来保护自己的隐私或秘密。 例如，你可能会用不许其他人看你的钱包、储物柜、房间或住宅这样的方式来保护某些隐私。一些政府机构禁止未授权的人进入某些特定建筑或军事基地，以此来保有隐私。

重点思考练习

辨别人们如何保护隐私

阅读以下改编自瓦里安·费赖伊的《拯救犹太人》的材料，区分人们保护某些隐私的不同方式，然后回答"你怎么看？"这一部分的问题，并准备与全班讨论自己的答案。

摘自：《拯救犹太人》

20 世纪 30 年代末，希特勒在德国的力量崛起和上台执政，对纳粹屠杀名单上数百万犹太人和其他人种来说标志着恐惧时代的来临。许多人逃往德国边境，试图越境去法国南部纳粹未占领的区域。但当法国在 1940 年 6 月向希特勒投降后，这些难民面临着被移交给盖世太保，并在集中营里被监禁、折磨和处决的危险。

一群对第三帝国的行为感到震惊的纽约人组成了紧急救援委员会。他们的目标是赶在盖世太保有所行动之前把那些艺术家、作家、音乐家、科学家、教授和政治人物运出法国。为此他们必须找到合适的人做中间人，这些人必须能自由出入法国，并愿意承担秘密使命所带来的危险。因此，一个没有任何特工经验的人——瓦里安·费赖伊，通过"国际基督教青年会"得到了很好的掩饰身份。通过他有效的地下工作，13 个月内有超过 1000 名难民成功地偷渡离开马赛。

"在我的三个助手——负责把风的比米什、负责面谈的弗兰西和秘书莉娜的帮助下，我们每天都会约见那些来寻求我们帮助的人。我们在白色档案卡片上记下他们的名字，但从来不写他们的地址。因为一旦警察突然袭击，写满了地址的卡片散落一地，这些人可能会被找到并被逮捕，这是我们所不想看到的。

In the evening, when all the refugees had finally gone, Beamish, Franzi, Lena, and I would hold a staff meeting.

We would go over all the cards for that day and try to decide what action to take on each case. Since we were always afraid the police might plant a hidden microphone in the room, we discussed all secret subjects in the bathroom, where we turned all the water faucets on full. We figured the noise of the water would make a recording sound like one long thunderstorm and not a word of what we said could be understood.

Secret subjects included false passports, false identity cards, false residence permits, and false safe-conduct passes. They also included secret escape routes over the Pyrenees Mountains into Spain and the names of those refugees who were in the greatest immediate danger from the Gestapo.

We couldn't cable these names to New York. We couldn't even mention them in a letter, because all letters were opened and read by a censor. So Lena typed out our secret messages on narrow sheets of thin paper. Then Beamish, Franzi, and I pasted the ends of the papers together and when the paste was dry, we made the long strips into tight rolls. We put each roll into a rubber finger and tied the end with a thin thread. Then we opened the bottom of a partly used tube of toothpaste or shaving cream. We pushed the rubber-covered packages well up into the tube. After we closed the end of the tube, we rolled it up a little way, so it would look as if it were in daily use. Whenever a refugee we trusted was leaving France, we sent the tube with him and asked him to mail the roll to New York when he reached Lisbon. All our secret messages got safely through to New York, and the police never caught on to our toothpaste trick.

How might wars or other conflicts require people to alter their privacy behavior? ☞

晚上所有难民都走了之后，比米什、弗兰西、莉娜和我会召开工作会议。

我们将仔细检查这一天记录的所有档案卡片，并讨论将对每一个案例采取哪一种拯救方案。由于我们总是害怕警察可能在房间里放置了隐藏的麦克风，我们会打开浴室里所有的水龙头，然后就在浴室里讨论所有秘密的内容。我们想，水的噪音会让录音听起来像一场漫长的雷雨，相反警察却听不到我们说的每个字。

保密的内容包括伪造的护照、身份证、居留许可和假的安全通行证；同时还包括翻越比利牛斯山脉进入西班牙的秘密逃生路线，和那些处于盖世太保威胁下最急切需要帮助的难民的名字。

因为所有信件都要被检查员打开和阅读，我们不能将这些名字发电报给纽约，我们甚至不能在任何通信中提到他们。因此莉娜会将我们的秘密消息打在一张窄窄的薄纸片上，然后比米什、弗兰西和我负责将纸条的两端粘在一起。粘胶干了之后，我们将长纸条紧紧地卷起来，然后将每个纸卷塞进橡胶指套里，并用细线将另一端扎紧。接着，把一管用过的牙膏或剃须膏从底部挖开，把用橡胶膜包好的纸卷塞进管里。封好之后，我们还会把牙膏管的尾部卷一卷，看上去好像是每天都在用的样子。每当有我们信任的难民要离开法国，我们就会将一管信息交给他，让他在到达里斯本后邮寄到纽约。警察从来没有截获过我们的牙膏信。

战争或其他冲突会怎样促使人们改变自己的隐私行为？

What do you think?

1.Who in the story wished to keep something private or secret?

2.What did they wish to keep secret?

3.From whom did they wish to keep something secret?

4.How did they behave to maintain privacy or keep secrets?

5.What examples in the story are there of the following:

• isolation

• secrecy

• confidentiality

• exclusion

Using the lesson

1. Draw a picture or make a collage to illustrate each of the four means described in this lesson that people use to maintain privacy: isolation, secrecy, confidentiality, and exclusion.

2. Why might it be important to protect from disclosure confidential communications, such as those with a doctor or lawyer? Are there any circumstances when such confidential communications should be disclosed? Explain your answer.

你怎么看?

1. 在这个故事中，谁希望保护某些隐私或要保密?

2. 他们希望保密的事情是什么?

3. 他们不希望这些秘密的事情让谁知道?

4. 他们怎样行动来保护隐私或保密?

5. 上述故事中包含了以下哪些情况:

- 隔离

- 秘密

- 私密

- 排斥

知识运用

1. 针对本课中所描述的人们用来保护隐私的四种方法:隔离、秘密、私密和排斥，分别画一幅图片或制作一幅拼贴画来说明。

2. 为什么对某些私密谈话（例如人们与医生或律师进行的交谈）的内容保密很重要? 哪些情况下应当披露这些私密谈话的内容? 请解释。

LESSON 3

Why Is Privacy Important to Individuals and to Institutions?

Purpose of Lesson

This lesson asks you to consider the importance of privacy for individuals and for institutions. You will have the opportunity to role-play a congressional hearing on the issue of press censorship during war time. When you have finished this lesson, you should be able to explain why individuals and institutions may wish to keep things secret.

Term to Know

institution

Critical Thinking Exercise

EXAMINING THE IMPORTANCE OF PRIVACY TO INDIVIDUALS

Poems, song lyrics, essays and other writings can make us think in new ways, or make us more aware of our own thoughts and feelings. As you read the following selections, think about the author's point of view. What is the author trying to tell us about privacy? Be prepared to share your thoughts with your class, then answer the "What do you think?" questions after discussing them with a study partner.

第三课：为什么隐私对个人和公共机构来说是重要的？

本课目标

本课要求你们思考隐私对个人和公共机构来说的重要性。你们将有机会进行角色扮演：针对战争时期的新闻审查问题举行一场模拟国会听证会。学完本课后，你们应当能够解释为什么个人和公共机构会希望对某些事情保密。

掌握词汇

公共机构

重要思考练习

考察隐私对个人的重要性

诗歌、歌曲的歌词、散文和其他文学作品可以让我们以新的方式进行思考，或让我们更了解自己的思想和感情。在阅读以下材料时，请思考原作者的创作意图。关于隐私，作者希望告诉我们什么？准备与全班分享你的想法，并与你的同学讨论后回答"你怎么看？"这一部分的问题。

1. From Something So Right

by Paul Simon (American songwriter, 1942-)

They got a wall in China!

It's a thousand miles long.

To keep out the foreigners they made it strong.

And I got a wall around me

That you can't even see.

It took a little time to get next to me.

2. From Mending Wall

by Robert Frost (American poet, 1874-1963)

Before I built a wall I'd ask to know

What I was walling in or walling out,

And to whom I was like to give offense.

Something there is that doesn't love a wall,

That wants it down.

Why is it important for people to have places to go where they can find privacy? ☞

1. **摘自《如此正确的事》**

   保罗·西蒙（美国词曲作者，1942—）

   在中国有个长城！

   它有一千英里长。

   为抵御外敌，人们把它建造得坚固又强大。

   环绕着我，也有一堵墙，你们甚至看不到。

   若要了解我，可要多花一点时间。

   歌词版权所有：1973。保罗·西蒙

2. **摘自《补墙》**

   罗伯特·弗罗斯特（美国诗人，1874—1963）

   我在造墙之前，先要弄个清楚，

   圈进来的是什么，圈出去的是什么，

   并且我可能得罪什么人。

   总有一些不喜欢墙的，要推倒它。

对人们来说，为什么能有一个隐私的去处是很重要的？

3. From Childe Harold's Pilgrimage

by Lord Byron (English poet, 1788-1824)

There is a pleasure in the pathless woods,

There is a rapture on the lonely shore,

There is society where none intrudes,

By the deep Sea, and music in its roar:

I love not Man the less, but Nature more,

From these our interviews, in which I steal

From all I may be or have been before,

To mingle with the Universe, and feel

What I can never express, yet cannot all conceal.

4. From Walden

by Henry David Thoreau (American essayist, 1817-1862)

My nearest neighbor is a mile distant, and no house is visible from any place but the hilltops within half a mile of my own. I have my horizon bounded by woods all to myself; a distant view of the railroad where it touches the pond on the one hand, and of the fence which skirts the woodland road on the other. But for the most part it is as solitary where I live as on the prairies. I have, as it were, my own sun and moon and stars, and a little world all to myself.

Men frequently say to me, I should think you feel lonesome down there, and want to be nearer to folks, rainy and snowy days and nights especially. [But] I find it wholesome to be alone the greater part of the time. To be in company, even with the best, is soon wearisome and dissipating. I love to be alone. I never found the companion that was so companionable as solitude.

Society is commonly too cheap. We meet at very short intervals, not having had time to acquire any new value for each other. We meet at the post-office, and at the sociable, and about the fireside every night; we live thick and are in each other's way, and stumble over one another, and I think that we thus lose some respect for one another.

3. **摘自《恰尔德·哈罗德尔游记》**

    拜伦勋爵（英国诗人，1788—1824）

    无径之林，常有情趣，

    无人之岸，几多惊喜，

    世外桃源，何处寻觅，

    聆听涛乐，须在海里；

    爱我爱你，更爱自然，

    摈弃自我，退身自思，

    拥抱自然，灵感如泉，

    面对自然，全无顾忌。

4. **摘自《瓦尔登湖》**

    亨利·大卫·梭罗（美国散文家，1817-1862）

　　最接近我的邻居在一英里外，看不到什么房子，除非独自登上那半里之外的小山山顶去望。我的地平线全给森林包围起来，专供我自个儿享受，极目远望只能望见那在湖的一端经过的铁路，和在湖的另一端沿着山林的公路边上的篱笆。大体说来，我居住的地方，寂寞得跟生活在大草原上一样。可以说，在这里我有我自己的太阳、月亮和星星，我有一个完全属于我自己的小世界。

　　人们常常对我说，"我想你在那儿住着一定觉得很寂寞吧，总是想要跟人们接近一下的吧，特别在下雨下雪的日子和夜晚。"（但）大部分时间里，我觉得寂寞是有益于健康的。有了伴儿，即使是最好的伴儿，不久也要厌倦，弄得很糟糕。我爱孤独（我喜欢独处）。我没有碰到比寂寞更好的同伴了。

　　社交往往过于廉价。我们相聚的时间是如此短促，都来不及使彼此获得任何新的有价值的东西。我们相会于邮局、各种社交场所，还有每晚在炉火边；我们生活得太拥挤，互相干扰，彼此牵绊，因此我想，我们已经缺乏了对彼此的敬意了。

What do you think?

1. What does Paul Simon think about the invisible walls around people? What purpose do they serve? What problems or disadvantages do they cause?

2. What does Robert Frost think the disadvantages are of building walls? What do you think the disadvantages are? What are the benefits?

3. What does Lord Byron think are the advantages of being alone? What does Henry Thoreau think? What do you think the advantages are? What are the disadvantages?

4. Do you ever try to keep a wall around you? When? What do you gain? What do you lose? Do you think you should try to keep a wall around you more often? Less often? Why?

5. Do you ever want to be alone? When? How do you feel when you want to be alone, but you can't?

6. Can you feel lonely even when you are around other people? What is the difference between being alone and being lonely?

Why is privacy important for institutions?

Just like privacy is important for individuals it also is important for some institutions. Institutions are established organizations, such as

• schools and universities

• business corporations

• museums

• hospitals

• federal, state, and local governments

你怎么看?

1. 保罗·西蒙如何看待人们周围看不见的墙?这些墙有什么用?这些墙带来了什么问题或缺点?

2. 罗伯特·弗罗斯特认为(在人与人之间)筑起一道墙有什么缺点?你觉得缺点是什么?有什么好处?

3. 拜伦认为独处的优势是什么?亨利·梭罗怎么想?你认为独处的优势是什么?缺陷又是什么?

4. 你是否曾经尝试在你周围筑起一道墙?那是在什么时候?你获得了什么?你失去了什么?你认为你应当更频繁地这么做吗?或者应该更少这么做?为什么?

5. 你是否曾经想过要独处?那是在什么时候?当你希望独处却做不到的时候,你会有什么感觉?

6. 你会感到孤独吗?即便是在周围有其他人的时候?独处和感觉孤独之间有什么区别?

为什么隐私对公共机构来说是重要的?

对某些公共机构来说,就如同对个人一样,隐私都是很重要的。这里的公共机构是指某些已经设立的组织和机构(基础性的组织),例如:

- 各级学校
- 企业公司
- 博物馆
- 医院
- 联邦、各州和地方政府

Some institutions have a need to keep certain things private. For example, hospitals keep medical records confidential; schools and universities keep student records confidential. Museums may want to keep their plans for buying new works of art private, and business corporations usually want to keep plans for new products and strategies for distributing and advertising them secret. Many governments have hidden weapons or secret military plans; they may have spies whose names are secret, and they often have letters and other documents that they want to keep top secret. In a democracy the government must be open to the people, but in the interest of national security some things must be kept private.

Critical Thinking Exercise

EVALUATING INSTITUTIONAL SECRECY

In this exercise the class is divided into groups to engage in a simulated congressional hearing on press censorship during wartime. First, read the following selection to find out what the military wanted to keep secret and why. Work in small groups to answer the "What do you think?" questions. Then follow the instructions in the next section to prepare for the hearing.

Congress Investigates Wartime Censorship

The Committee on Government Affairs of the United States Senate has decided to hold a hearing to investigate the extent to which the military should be able to censor the press during wartime. Witnesses from the Department of Defense and the news media have been asked to testify.

What is the reason for the hearing? During the 1991 war in the Persian Gulf, a number of reporters complained that the Department of Defense was placing too many restrictions on the news media. In the battlefield area, reporters were assigned to small groups or pools that military officers had to escort at all times. They could only go where the military guides took them. Reporters had to submit their battlefield stories to military officers for review before publication. If the military officers found information they thought might aid the enemy, they cut it out of the stories. Some of the military escorts may have been overly strict in supervising the reporters.

　　某些公共机构需要对某些特定事情保密。例如：医院要对医疗记录保密；学校和大学要对学生的记录和档案保密；博物馆可能不想要曝光即将购买新艺术品的计划；企业公司通常将新产品、产品销售及广告计划视为商业秘密。许多国家的政府机构都有秘密的武器或军事计划，也有秘密的间谍名单，也通常需要对信函和其他文件保密。在民主体制中，所有政府部门都必须向民众公开，但出于国家安全的利益考虑，某些事情则必须保密。

重点思考练习

评估公共机构的秘密

　　在本次练习中，针对战争时期的新闻审查问题，全班将分组进行一场模拟国会听证会。首先，请阅读以下材料，找出军方希望保密的内容以及原因。各小组讨论回答"你怎么看？"这一部分的问题。然后按照下一节中的听证会说明，为模拟听证会做准备。

国会调查战时新闻审查

　　美国参议院的政府事务委员会决定举行一场听证会，以调查在多大程度上军方应当可以在战争时期对新闻媒体的报道进行审查。听证会也邀请了来自国防部和新闻媒体界的人士出席作证。

　　为什么要举行这场听证会？在 1991 年波斯湾战争期间，很多记者抱怨国防部过多地限制了新闻媒体。在战场，记者们被分成了很少人的小组或团体，随时都有军事人员跟随。他们只能去军方的向导带他们去的地方。记者们必须要将他们的战地报道在出版前交给军方审查。如果军方审查人员发现任何他们认为可能会有助于敌军的信息，就会截断并阻止这则报道刊登。某些军方随从人员还会过分严格地监视记者的行动。

Military censorship procedures had been different in the past. For example, during World War II, reporters had been free to travel anywhere and see anything. Then they wrote their stories and submitted them to the military censor. The censor took out any information that might be helpful to the enemy; the rest was published.

During the Persian Gulf War reporters were not free to travel wherever and whenever they wanted. Reporters were told what they could not see instead of what they could not report. Arguably, this system did not allow reporters to gather information and report it properly. Limitations on access to information was a far more serious form of censorship which made it more difficult for the American public to decide whether the news reports were accurate and trustworthy.

On the other hand, from a military standpoint the press had sent too many reporters to the region to be handled effectively. Moreover, reporters often asked questions during televised briefings that the military could not answer without endangering the troops. Additionally, live satellite transmissions and other modern technologies involved in newsgathering during the Persian Gulf War made it impossible to allow reporters the freedom they enjoyed in the pre-television days of World War II.

What do you think?

1. What did the military want to keep secret?
2. From whom did the military wish to keep the information secret?
3. How did the military plan to keep the information secret?
4. Why did the military want to keep the information secret?

 What information about events during the Persian Gulf War (1991) should have been shared by General Norman Schwartzkopf with members of the press? What information should have been with held? ☞

　　如今的军事审查程序和过去大有不同。例如在第二次世界大战期间，记者们可以自由地前往任何地方，观察任何事件，然后写出自己的报道，并提交给军方审查。审查员删掉任何可能有助于敌人的信息，文稿的其他部分仍然可以出版。

　　在波斯湾战争期间，记者不能按照自己的意愿去任何地方或决定什么时间去。记者被告知"不许看"，而并非"不许报道"。可以说，这种规定不允许记者收集资料和进行适当的报道。对信息获取渠道的限制这种更加严格的审查形式，使美国公众更难判断新闻报道是否准确和可靠。

　　另一方面，从军方的角度来看，媒体派出太多新闻记者前往该地区，导致事态无法得到有效的处理。此外，记者经常在电视简报会议上提出某些危及部队安全并导致军方无法回答的问题。此外，在海湾战争时期，新闻采访中所用到的卫星传输现场直播和其他现代技术，使记者们无法再享受到电视机诞生前的第二次世界大战时期所拥有的那种自由。

你怎么看？

1. 军方希望保密的事情是什么？
2. 军方希望这些信息对谁保密？
3. 军方打算如何保护有关这些信息的秘密？
4. 军方希望对这些消息保密的原因是什么？

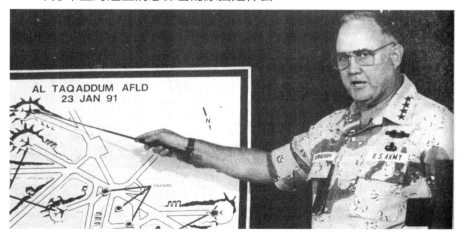

在1991年波斯湾战争当中，诺曼·施瓦茨科普夫将军应当向新闻媒体透露什么信息？不应当透露哪些信息？

Preparing for the Hearing

To prepare for the hearing, the class should be divided into five groups, with each group assigned to play one of the following roles:

- Department of Defense: You will seek to justify the restrictions placed on the press by the military.

- Coalition of Radio and Television Broadcasters: You will seek the broadest possible freedom to observe and report the news as it happens.

- Associated Press (AP): Your members are news paper and magazine reporters who seek complete freedom of access to information on the condition that they submit their stories to a military censor before publication.

- Center for National Defense Policy Studies: Your group generally uses arguments based on practical necessity to support the military's point of view.

- Senate Committee on Government Affairs: As elected representatives of the people of the United States, you seek to make the best decision possible for the good of the country. You will listen carefully to all sides and attempt to resolve this privacy issue wisely, keeping in mind both the need for national security and the people's right to know.

The first four groups should prepare a three-minute presentation explaining and justifying their position on what role the military should have in censoring the press during wartime. Each group should select one or two spokespersons to present its position to the committee, but all group members should be prepared to assist in answering the committee's questions.

准备听证会

为了准备听证会，全班应分为五组，分别扮演以下角色之一：

国防部：你们将设法证明军方制约新闻媒体的正确性。

广播电台和电视台联盟：你们将争取获得尽可能更广泛的自由，观察和报道正在发生的事件并制作新闻。

联合新闻社（美联社）：你们是新闻报纸和杂志的记者，希望争取获得信息的完全自由，前提是在发表之前将自己的报道提交给一位军方审查员审查。

国防政策研究中心：你们组通常采用基于实际需要的论据来支持军方的观点。

参议院政府事务委员会：作为美国人民选出的代表，你们要争取做出符合国家利益的最佳决定。你们需要认真聆听来自各方的声音，并要明智地解决这个有关隐私的问题。要记住，需要同时考虑到国家安全和人民的知情权。

前四个小组应当各自准备一段三分钟的发言，针对"战争时期军方应当在审查新闻媒体中扮演怎样的角色"这一问题做出回答，并解释和论证自己的答案。每个小组都要选出一到两个发言人向第五组的政府事务委员会陈述自己小组的观点。但所有小组成员都应当准备协助发言人回答委员会提出的问题。

While the first four groups are preparing their presentations, the Senate Committee on Government Affairs should prepare questions to ask each group, and should select a chairperson to conduct the hearing.

Conducting the Hearing

The chairperson of the Senate Committee on Government Affairs should call the hearing to order. Each group should be given three minutes to present its arguments, followed by three minutes of questioning by members of the committee. After all four groups have completed their testimony, members of the committee should discuss the arguments presented and attempt to reach a consensus on how to deal with this privacy issue. The committee's deliberations should be conducted in front of the class, and the committee should propose a formal resolution that sets forth their decision on the extent to which the military should be allowed to censor the press during wartime.

Using the Lesson

1. What other institutions might have information about people that they want to keep secret? What kind of information might they want to keep secret? Why?

2. What information might you want that an institution could refuse to give to you because it is secret? Should it be kept secret? Why?

3. Do you think there are some kinds of information that our government should be allowed to keep secret? What are some reasons the government might want to keep a secret? Do you think there are some kinds of information that the government should not be allowed to keep secret, even if it wants to? Explain your position.

在前四个小组准备各自的发言时，第五组"参议院政府事务委员会"应当准备好要问每一个小组的问题，并选出一位代表担任委员会主席，主持听证会。

召开听证会

第五组"参议院政府事务委员会"的主席宣布听证会正式开始。每个小组都有三分钟时间进行陈述，接着各有三分钟用来回答委员会成员提出的质询。所有四组完成发言后，委员会成员应讨论各组所提出的论据，并对如何处理这一隐私问题达成共识。委员会的审议过程应当在全班面前进行。最后，委员会应当提出一项正式决议，针对战争时期允许军方审查新闻媒体的程度问题，对委员会的最后决定进行说明。

知识运用

1. 还有其他哪些公共机构会有人们希望保密的信息？哪些种类的信息是人们希望保密的？为什么？

2. 有什么信息是你想要知道、但某个公共机构会因为它是保密信息而拒绝提供给你的？这个信息应当被保密吗？为什么？

3. 你认为是否存在某些应当允许政府保密的信息？政府想要对这些信息保密可能出于哪些原因？你认为是否存在某些信息，即便政府想要对此保密，但也不应当允许？解释你的观点。

Unit Two
What Factors Explain Differences in Privacy Behavior?

Purpose of Unit

This unit will introduce you to the factors that explain differences in the privacy behavior of individual. You will learn that although privacy exists in all societies and cultures, there are often differences in the privacy behavior of individuals within a society and between different societies. You will examine some areas in which differences are common as well as the reasons for these differences.

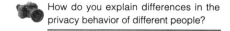 How do you explain differences in the privacy behavior of different people?

第二单元：哪些因素可以解释隐私行为之间的差异？

单元目标

　　本单元将向你们介绍某些可以解释个人隐私行为之间差异的因素。你们会学到：尽管隐私存在于所有社会和不同的文化背景中，但无论是在同一个社会里，还是不同的社会之间，个人的隐私行为都往往大不相同。你们将研究个人的隐私行为通常出现差异的地方和产生差异的原因。

如何解释不同个人的隐私行为之间的差异？

LESSON 4
Why Might People's Privacy Behavior Differ?

Purpose of Lesson

This lesson examines some of the common reasons for the differences in privacy behavior among people. When you have finished this lesson, you should be able to describe and explain similarities and differences in privacy behavior.

Terms to Know

factor	occupation
role	values

Critical Thinking Exercise

EXAMINING PRIVACY BEHAVIOR

As you read the following excerpt from "A Journey," a short story by the American writer Edith Wharton (1862-1937), identify examples of the main character's privacy behavior. Then work with a study partner to answer the "What do you think?" questions. Be prepared to share your answers with the class.

A Journey

The sleeping car had sunk into its night silence. Through the wet windowpane she watched the sudden lights, the long stretches of hurrying blackness. Now and then she turned her head and looked through the opening in the hangings at her husband's curtains across the aisle. She wondered restlessly if he wanted anything and if she could hear him if he called. His voice had grown very weak within the last months and it irritated him when she did not hear.... She crept to the dressing room. When she had washed her face and adjusted her dress she felt more hopeful.... In ten hours they would be at home!

第四课：为什么人们的隐私行为会有不同？

本课目标

　　本课探讨了人们的隐私行为之所以不同的某些常见原因。学完本课后，你们应当能够描述和解释隐私行为之间的相似和差异之处。

掌握词汇

因素	职业
角色	价值

重点思考练习

研究隐私行为

　　阅读以下改编自美国作家伊迪斯・华顿夫人（1862-1937）的短篇小说《一段旅程》的材料，找出小说主角的隐私行为。与一位同学合作回答"你怎么看？"这一部分的问题，并准备与全班分享你们的答案。

《一段旅程》

　　沉睡的车厢陷入了夜晚的宁静。透过潮湿的玻璃窗她看到了突如其来的光，黑暗中匆匆留下了长长的影子，她立刻转过头，看着走道对面丈夫的床帘顶端的空隙。她不安地想着他是否需要什么，她是否能听到他的呼唤。最近几个月他的声音变得很微弱，如果她没有听到他就会勃然大怒……她悄悄地走进更衣室，洗完脸，整了整裙子，顿时觉得仿佛充满了希望……10个小时后他们就能到家了！

She stepped to her husband's berth. She leaned over him and drew up the shade. As she did so she touched one of his hands. It felt cold.... She bent closer, laying her hand on his arm and calling him by name. He did not move.

She gently shook his shoulder. He lay motionless. She caught hold of his hand again: it slipped from her limply, like a dead thing. A dead thing?

She leaned forward, and shrinkingly, with a sickening reluctance, laid her hands on his shoulders and turned him over. His head fell back; his face looked small and smooth; he gazed at her with steady eyes.

She remained motionless for a long time, holding him. Suddenly she shrank back: the longing to scream, to call out, to fly from him, had almost overpowered her. But a strong hand arrested her. Good God! If it were known that he was dead they would be put off the train at the next station.

In a terrifying flash of remembrance there arose before her a scene she had once witnessed in traveling, when a husband and wife, whose child had died on the train, had been thrust out at some chance station. She saw them standing on the platform with the child's body between them. And this was what would happen to her. Within the next hour she might find herself on the platform of some strange station, alone with her husband's body.... It was too horrible.

 What reasons might the woman in this story have to conceal her husband's unexpected death in their private berth aboard this passenger train? ☞

　　她走到丈夫的铺位旁边，俯身靠近他，她的影子投射在他的身上。她摸了摸他的手，是冰凉的……她弯下腰靠得更近，抓住他的胳膊，叫着他的名字。但他并没有动。

　　她轻轻地摇了摇他的肩膀，他躺在那里一动不动。她再次抓住了他的手，它软绵绵地滑落了下去，仿佛没有生命的物体。"没有生命的物体？"

　　她瑟缩着俯身向前，忍不住有些作呕，但还是将手放在他的肩膀上，把他翻了过来。他的头向后倒下，他的脸看上去小而光滑，眼睛定定地凝视着她。

　　有很长时间，她呆住了，一动不动地一直抱着他。突然，她害怕地瑟缩起来：打从心里想要尖叫出声，飞一般从他身边逃走，这些想法几乎吞没了她，但有一双更有力的手按住了她。天哪！如果有人知道他死了，他们会被要求在下一站就下车。

　　她的脑中迅速闪过一段可怕的回忆：在某次旅行中她看到一对夫妻的孩子死在了火车上，在某个不知名的小站全家人被赶下了车。她看到他们站在站台上，孩子的尸体就放在旁边。现在，这场景可能就要发生在她的身上。再接下来的一个小时后，她可能会发现自己身处一个陌生的车站，独自和她丈夫的尸体待在一起……这太可怕了。

可能出于什么原因，故事里的女主人公隐瞒了她的丈夫意外死在这辆旅客列车的私人铺位的事实？

She felt the train moving more slowly. They were approaching a station! With a violent gesture she drew down the shade to hide her husband's face.

Feeling dizzy, she sank down on the edge of the berth, keeping away from his outstretched body, and pulling the curtains close, so that he and she were shut into a kind of twilight.... She tried to think. At all costs she must conceal the fact that he was dead. But how?

She heard the porter making up her bed; people were beginning to move about the car. With a supreme effort she rose to her feet, stepping into the aisle of the car and drawing the curtains tight behind her. She noticed that they still parted slightly with the motion of the car, and finding a pin in her dress she fastened them together. Now she was safe....

The porter, moving to and fro under his burden of sheets and pillows, glanced at her as he passed.

At length he said: "Ain't he going to get up? We're ordered to make up the berths as early as we can."

She turned cold with fear. They were just entering the station. "oh, not yet," she stammered. "Not till he's had his milk. Won't you get it, please?"

"All right. Soon as we start again."

When the train moved on he reappeared with the milk. She took it from him and sat vaguely looking at it. At length she became aware that the porter still hovered expectantly.

 How does the character in this story behave to maintain the secret of her husband's death aboard the passenger train? ☞

　　她觉得列车开得越来越慢，火车正在靠近站台！她猛地用某种粗鲁的姿势挡住了丈夫的脸。

　　她感到一阵头晕目眩，昏倒在床铺边，离他直挺挺的身体远远的，把床帘紧紧拉上，这样他和她就完全笼罩在某种阴暗死寂的光线中……她开始努力思考：她必须不惜一切代价隐瞒他已经死去的事实，但是该怎么做呢？

　　她听到列车员在整理她的床铺，人们开始在车厢里走来走去。使出了全身力气，她站起来向过道走去，将她身后的帘子紧紧地拉上。她注意到随着列车的移动，帘子之间还有些缝隙，她在自己的裙子上找到了一个别针，将帘子穿在一起。现在她安全了……

　　列车员在他的铺位前来回走动，间或看她一眼。

　　最后他说："他不打算起床吗？我们要尽快整理完所有床铺。"此时的她正因为恐惧而全身冰凉，火车才刚刚进站。"喔，还没有"，她结结巴巴地说："他要等喝了牛奶再起来，可以帮我们拿一瓶来吗？"

　　"好的，等车开动后我就拿来。"

　　火车再次启动后，列车员拿着牛奶过来了，她从他手上接过瓶子坐下来，恍惚地瞪着那瓶牛奶。终于她意识到，列车员还站在一边等着她。

这个故事的女主人公如何努力隐瞒她丈夫死在火车上的秘密？

'Will I give it to him?" he suggested. "Oh, no," she cried, rising. "He, he's asleep yet, I think."

She waited until the porter had passed on; then she unpinned the curtains and slipped behind them. In the semi-obscurity her husband's face stared up at her like a marble mask with agate eyes. She put out her hand and drew down the lids. Then she remembered the glass of milk: what was she to do with it? She thought of throwing it out the window; but to do so she would have to lean across his body and bring her face close to his. She decided to drink the milk.

After a while the porter came back. 'When'll I fold up his bed?" he asked. "Oh, not yet; he's ill, he's very ill. Can't you let him stay as he is?" He took the empty milk glass and walked away....

Suddenly she found herself picturing what would happen when the train reached New York. She shuddered as it occurred to her that he would be quite cold and that someone might perceive he had been dead since morning.

She thought, "If they see I am not surprised they will suspect something. They will ask questions, and if I tell them the truth they won't believe me, no one would believe me! It will be terrible. I must pretend I don't know. When they open the curtains I must go up to him quite naturally, and then I must scream" She had an idea that the scream would be very hard to do.

What do you think?

1.What does the main character try to keep private?

2.How does the main character behave-what does she do-to maintain privacy?

3.Are these behaviors examples of isolation, secrecy, confidentiality, or exclusion?

4.How do you explain the main character's privacy behavior? Why does she attempt to maintain privacy as she does?

"需要我递给他吗？"他提议。"哦，不用，"她提高了音量："他，他还在睡呢，我想。"

她一直等到列车员走开，才取下床帘上的别针，悄悄爬进去。朦胧中她丈夫的脸正对着她，那对眼睛就像是大理石面具上的玛瑙珠子。她伸出手将他的眼睑轻轻合上。然后她想起了那瓶牛奶，她应该怎么办呢？她想把它扔出窗外；但那样她需要俯身靠近他，他们会脸对着脸。想了想，她还是决定把牛奶喝掉。

过了一会儿，列车员回来了。"我什么时候来给他收床？"他问。"噢，现在还不用，他病了，病得很厉害，你能不能让他就这样待着？"列车员拿着那牛奶空瓶走开了……

突然，她发现自己在想象当火车到达纽约后即将要发生的事，不禁打了一个寒颤。她想到，他的身体那时会非常冰凉，会让人觉得他早上就已经死了。

她想："如果他们看到我并不惊讶，就会对我产生怀疑，他们会问我问题。而如果我告诉他们真相，他们不会相信我，没有人会相信我！这太可怕了！我必须假装我不知道，当他们一拉开床帘，我要马上很自然地走到他的床边，然后我要大声尖叫！"她想，要发出那一声尖叫该有多么困难。

你怎么看？

1. 故事主人公试图保密的事情是什么？
2. 故事主人公如何保护自己的隐私（她做了什么）？
3. 这些行为属于隔离、秘密、私密还是排斥？
4. 如何解释故事主人公的隐私行为？她为什么要这样努力保护自己的隐私？

What factors influence privacy behavior?

People often differ in the objects they wish to keep private and in the ways they behave to keep these objects secret. How can we explain these differences? Various factors, or elements, in people's lives explain differences in their privacy behavior. The following are some factors that typically influence a person's privacy behavior:

1. Family. A person's family environment may influence his or her privacy behavior. For example:

- In LaToya's family, no one ever talks about Uncle Hubert, especially in front of Grandma, because he became severely depressed and committed suicide several years ago.

- Oksana and hers even bother sand sisters live with their grandparents in a tiny apartment. It is very crowded and no one has a private space to call their own. Oksana dreams of having her own room where she can be alone.

2. Occupation or role. A person's job or role may require him or her to maintain privacy. For example:

- Michael is a famous professional athlete. To avoid being harassed by reporters and mobbed by fans, Michael keeps his home address and telephone number confidential.

- Sonya works in product development for a large corporation. She is sworn to secrecy and cannot discuss her work with her friends.

3. Individual experiences. Past experiences may influence how a person wants to live to maintain privacy. For example:

- A friend Frank trusted embarrassed him several years ago when he revealed to the whole class something Frank had whispered in confidence. Since then, Frank has not trusted anyone to keep a secret, and he keeps his private thoughts to himself.

- Martina's family always discussed their problems openly. When Martina became an adult, there were very few things she would not discuss with her friends.

4. Opportunities for privacy. People's behavior may be influenced by the opportunities for privacy that exist in their environment. For example:

影响隐私行为的因素有哪些?

人们希望保密的内容往往不同,人们保护这些隐私所使用的行为方式也是不同的。我们要如何解释这些差异呢?人们的生活中有各种因素或元素,都可以用来解释个人隐私行为之间的差异。以下是一些影响个人隐私行为的典型因素:

1. **家庭**:一个人的家庭环境可能会影响他或她的隐私行为。例如:

   在拉托雅家里,从来没有人提到休伯特叔叔,特别是在奶奶面前。因为几年前他患上严重的抑郁症后自杀了。

   奥克萨纳、她的 7 个兄弟姐妹和他们的祖父母住在一间很小的公寓里。家里非常拥挤,谁也没有属于自己的私人空间。奥克萨纳梦想着有一天她能拥有自己的房间,她能独自一个人住。

2. **职业或角色**:一个人的工作或角色可能要求他或她保护隐私。例如:

   迈克尔是一名著名的职业运动员。为了避免被记者和球迷围攻骚扰,迈克尔一直对自己的家庭住址和电话号码保密。

   索尼娅在一家大公司负责产品开发,她曾起誓要对工作内容保密,不能与她的朋友讨论她的工作。

3. **个人经历**:过去的经历可能会对个人如何保护隐私权的生活方式产生影响。例如:

   几年前,一个弗兰克信任的朋友曾让他很难堪,他把弗兰克私下里告诉他的事情说给全班同学听。从那时起,弗兰克不再相信有任何人可以保守秘密,除了他自己,没有人知道他的想法。

   玛蒂娜的家人常常公开讨论家里的问题,所以马丁娜成年后,几乎所有事情她都会跟她的朋友们讨论。

4. **保护隐私的机会**:周围环境中是否存在保护隐私的机会,对人们的行为可能会有影响。例如:

- In his book 1984, George Orwell described a society in which there was a special television screen (telescreen) in every home. This telescreen allowed the government to watch and listen to everything people did. The main character, Winston Smith, found a tiny room above a shop that did not have a telescreen. Even though it was small and run-down, it was like paradise for Winston.

- Many people who live in large cities find privacy in the anonymous crowds of people.

5. Value placed on privacy. People's behavior may differ depending on the value they, their family, or their culture place on privacy. For example:

- Some people who grow up in small towns have neighbors that share everything that happens in their lives.

6. Competing values. Although people may value privacy highly, sometimes other things may be more important to them in specific situations. For example:

- In The Adventures of Tom Sawyer by Mark Twain, Tom and Huck swore to each other that they would never tell anyone about the murder they witnessed. But after searching his conscience, Tom decided to testify to save a man wrongly accused of the crime.

7. Individual differences sometimes lead people to make **different choices** with regard to privacy. For example:

- Jamal and Eli are students at Central High. They each have many friends and enjoy talking with them. Jamal does not mind telling his friends just about anything. On the other hand, Eli keeps some things to himself.

Critical Thinking Exercise

IDENTIFYING THE FACTORS THAT INFLUENCE PRIVACY BEHAVIOR

Work with a study partner to answer the following questions. You may use the examples of privacy behavior you have just read, or examples from your experience or imagination, to explain your answers. Be prepared to discuss your answers with the class.

乔治·奥威尔在他的小说《1984》中，曾描述过这样一个社会：每家每户都有一个特别的电视屏幕，透过这块屏幕，政府能够看到或听到人们做的每件事。故事的主人公温斯顿·史密斯发现了一家商店楼上的小房间里没有这种电视屏幕，因此，虽然这房间很小且残破不堪，但对主人公温斯顿来说却如同天堂一般。

住在大城市里的许多人在陌生人群中找到隐私。

5. **对隐私的重视程度**：人们的行为可能会由于他们、他们的家庭或文化对隐私态度的不同而不同。例如：

有些在小城镇中生活的人，邻里之间会把生活中发生的所有事情都拿来分享。

6. **冲突的价值观**：尽管人们已经非常重视隐私，但有时在某些特定场合下，可能有其他事情对人们来说比隐私更重要。例如：

在马克·吐温的小说《汤姆·索亚历险记》中，汤姆和哈克曾对彼此发誓永远不会把他们目睹的那场谋杀案告诉任何人。但为了解救一个被误认为犯有谋杀罪被起诉的人，面对自己的良心，汤姆还是决定出庭作证。

7. **个体差异有时会让人们在隐私问题上做出不同的选择。** 例如：

贾马尔和以利都是中心高中的学生，他们都有很多朋友，并喜欢与朋友们聊天。贾马尔并不介意跟他的朋友们讨论任何事，但以利会保留一些自己的秘密。

重点思考练习

找出影响隐私行为的因素

与一位同学一起讨论并回答下列问题。你们可以运用上文中提到的隐私行为的案例，或是从自己的经历或想象中寻找案例来解释你们的答案。准备与全班讨论。

1.How might a person's family environment and past experiences influence his or her privacy behavior?

2.How might a person's occupation or role require him or her to maintain privacy?

3.How might differences in people's values explain differences in their privacy behavior?

4.How might differences in the opportunities for privacy explain differences in privacy behavior?

Critical Thinking Exercise

EVALUATING HOW DIFFERENT OCCUPATIONS INFLUENCE PRIVACY BEHAVIOR

In this exercise your class will role-play two TV talk show discussions. The subject is the influence of different occupations on privacy behavior. Half the class-Group A-will examine how certain occupations influence a person's privacy needs, and half the class-Group B -will examine how certain other occupations require a person to intrude on-or to protect-the privacy of others. One or two students from each group should be assigned the role of interviewer, to lead and moderate the discussion and to ask questions of the other group members.

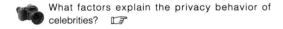 What factors explain the privacy behavior of celebrities? ☞

1. 一个人的家庭环境和过去的经历是怎样影响他或她的隐私行为的？
2. 一个人的职业或角色需要他或她怎样保护隐私？
3. 怎样用人们价值观的差异来解释他们隐私行为上的差异？
4. 怎样用保护隐私的机会不同来解释隐私行为之间的差异？

重点思考练习

评估不同的职业如何影响隐私行为

本次练习中，全班将进行角色扮演，模拟进行两个电视谈话节目，主题是不同职业对隐私行为的影响。全班的一半组成 A 组，研究某种职业如何影响个人的隐私需求；另外一半同学组成 B 组，研究其他职业如何需要个人侵犯（或保护）他人的隐私。每组各有一到两名同学担任采访者的角色，引导和主持小组讨论，并向对方组员提问。

哪些因素可以用来解释名人的隐私行为呢？

Group A-Members of this group should be assigned to play the role of one of the following occupations, and should be prepared to describe how their occupation influences their need for privacy:

• magician
• movie actor/actress
• inventor
• politician
• writer
• lawyer

Group B-Members of this group should be assigned to play the role of one of the following occupations, and should be prepared to explain how their occupation requires them to intrude on, and to protect, the privacy of others:

• newspaper reporter
• talk show host
• police officer
• doctor
• private investigator
• psychiatrist

Group B should play the role of studio audience during the presentation by Group A and vice versa.

Using the Lesson

1. How does your privacy behavior compare with the privacy behavior described in the examples in this? What factors explain the similarities and differences?

2. What factors explain the differences between your privacy behavior and that of your friends? What factors explain the similarities?

3. Should people in certain jobs-top athletes or public officials, for example-be allowed less privacy than the rest of us? Why or why not?

A 组：该组成员选择扮演以下职业中一种，并准备描述这种职业是如何影响他们对隐私的需求的：

- 魔术师
- 电影演员
- 发明家
- 政治人物
- 作家
- 律师

B 组：该组成员选择扮演以下职业中的一种，并准备解释这种职业是如何要求他们侵犯和保护他人隐私的：

- 新闻记者
- 谈话节目主持人
- 警察
- 医生
- 私人侦探
- 心理医生

在 A 组进行陈述的时候，B 组应扮演观众的角色，反之亦然。

知识运用

1. 怎样把你的隐私行为与本课案例中描述的隐私行为进行比较？哪些因素可以用来解释它们之间的相似和差异之处？
2. 哪些因素可以解释你和你的朋友们在隐私行为上的差异？哪些因素可以解释它们之间的相同之处？
3. 某些从事特定职业的人（例如顶尖运动员或政府官员）应该比我们其他人拥有更少的隐私吗？为什么？为什么不？

LESSON 5

How Do Different Societies Deal with Privacy?

Purpose of Lesson

This lesson provides an opportunity to examine some ways that different societies, and different generations in the same society, deal with privacy. When you have finished this lesson, you should be able to explain societal similarities and differences in privacy behavior.

What differences exist among societies in the way they maintain privacy?

Privacy is found in all societies. People of different societies, however, may differ in the objects they choose to keep private and the means they use to maintain privacy. Even within one society, people of different generations may have very different privacy behavior. For example, some people think their age should be kept private. Others may reveal their age, but not feel comfortable revealing their religious or political beliefs. In some cultures, people always eat in private; it is considered indecent to eat in public.

People also may differ in the ways they maintain privacy. For example, the people in some societies build homes with soundproof walls to promote. privacy. In other societies, walls may be thin and sound can easily travel through them. In such societies, people maintain a sense of privacy by purposely not listening or by pretending not to overhear one another.

Societies can be complicated. In some cases, people of one society might be uncomfortable if they are more than one foot away from others while talking to them. On the other hand, people from another society might be uncomfortable if others are less than one foot from them. What do you think might happen when people from these different societies talk to each either?

In the following exercises you will examine similarities and differences in the privacy behavior of people from different generations and different societies.

第五课：不同的文化如何处理隐私问题？

本课目标

　　本课让我们有机会探讨某些不同社会、或同一社会中不同时代的人处理隐私问题的方式。学完本课后，你们应该能够解释隐私行为在社会属性上的相似和差异之处。

不同社会在保护隐私的方式上有什么不同？

　　所有社会都存在隐私。不同社会的人们会选择对不同的内容保密，他们用来保护隐私的手段也不尽相同。即使是在同一个社会中，不同时代的人可能有非常不一样的隐私行为，例如，有些人认为自己的年龄应当保密，而有些人虽然不介意透露自己的年纪，却不愿意表露自己的宗教或政治信仰。在某些文化中，人们总是在私密的地方吃饭，在公共场合吃东西被认为是不文雅的。

　　人们保护隐私的方式也有不同。例如，某些社会中人们在建造房屋的时候会使用隔音墙，以便更好地保护隐私。而在其他某些社会中，墙壁可能很薄，声音可以轻易穿透，人们会刻意不去听或假装没有听到彼此的声音，以保持一种隐私感。

　　社会是很复杂的。在某些情况下，某个社会的人可能会因为和相距一英尺之外的其他人说话而觉得不自在，另一个社会的人对不到一英尺的交谈距离又会感到不舒服。试着想象一下，来自以上这两种不同社会的人相互交谈时，可能会发生什么事？

　　接下来的练习中，你们会研究不同时代和不同社会的人在隐私行为方面的相似和不同之处。

Critical Thinking Exercise

EXAMINING PRIVACY IN ANOTHER CULTURE

Read the following selection carefully. As you do, try to identify the privacy behavior of the Zuni and think about what might account for this behavior. Answer the "What do you think?" questions. Be prepared to discuss your answers with the class.

Privacy and the Zuni

The Zuni are a tribe of American Indians who live in the southwestern United States. Generally, the Zuni live in large houses. Each house is for an extended family. When the daughters of a family are married they bring their husbands to live in the family home. A typical eight-room house for twenty or so people has four rooms for common use-a living room, a kitchen, a storeroom, and a workroom. Each of the married daughters has a bedroom/workroom for herself and her family. The rooms are linked by connecting doors and interior windows. The approach area to each house is watched by family members. This is done so that whenever someone comes to visit, the family can be prepared. In this way the activities of the family can be kept private.

 What factors help explain the different ways in which the Zuni people maintain their privacy behavior? ☞

重点思考练习

研究不同文化的隐私

仔细阅读下面的材料，试着找出属于祖尼人隐私行为的案例，思考可以解释这种隐私行为的因素。回答"你怎么看？"这一部分的问题。准备与全班讨论你的答案。

祖尼人和隐私

祖尼人是生活在美国西南部的一个美洲印第安人部落。通常，祖尼人都是几代同堂的大家族一起住在大房子里。家族中有女儿结婚时，她们会把自己的丈夫带回家里住。每个大房子里通常有八个房间，容纳20多个人同住，其中有四个房间做日常使用：一间起居室、一间厨房、一间储藏室和一个工作室。每个已婚的女儿都有一间自己和家人的卧室或工作室。每个房间通过门和室内窗户相连通。大房子的门厅通常由家族成员轮流照看，这是为了有访客来的时候全家都可以有所准备。通过这种方式可以保持家庭活动的私密性。

哪些因素能用来解释祖尼人保护自己隐私行为的不同方式？

The most private areas of a Zuni household are the storeroom and the storage areas within each bedroom where sacred religious objects are kept. These objects are considered to be very powerful. Members of the tribe who are not authorized to use sacred objects are afraid even to handle them. Even the rooms in which they are kept are taboo to visitors.

When these objects are used in religious rituals, the greatest secrecy is in effect. All unauthorized Zuni and foreigners are forbidden to be in the area. This is essential so that religious activities can be conducted without interference and so that information about them will not be revealed.

There are many methods for maintaining the secrecy of these religious objects and rituals. Looking in through the windows of houses, especially at night, is not permitted. In 1890, two people who looked in through the windows at night were considered to be witches and were tried and beaten. Even today, most Zuni houses have outdoor lights for night surveillance and guard dogs to warn of intruders. When rituals are in progress, security is maintained by people standing guard inside and outside the room. It is also maintained by solid walls. In addition, customary respect for the taboos and ordinary good manners help preserve privacy and secrecy in the Zuni village.

What do you think?

1. What are the objects of privacy or secrecy for the Zuni?

2. From whom are these objects of privacy kept private or secret?

3. How do the Zuni behave to keep these objects of privacy secret, that is, to maintain privacy with regard to these things?

4. Why do you suppose the Zuni seek privacy with regard to these things?

Critical Thinking Exercise

IDENTIFYING DIFFERENCES IN PRIVACY BEHAVIOR

Read the following selection carefully. As you do, identify the differences in privacy behavior the author describes among people of different societies and different generations. Then answer the "What do you think?" questions. Be prepared to discuss your answers with the class.

祖尼人家庭中最私密的地方是房子里的储藏室和每个卧室中的储物区，那里通常放置着神圣的宗教物品，而祖尼人认为这些宗教物品拥有强大的力量。如果没有事先得到授权使用这些圣物，部落成员甚至都不敢触摸它们。即使是放在房间里，访客也不允许接近它们。

当这些圣物用于宗教仪式的时候，保密程度也上升到最高级别。所有未被授权的祖尼人和外人都被禁止进入正在进行仪式的区域。至关重要的是要保证宗教活动不受干扰，仪式信息不被泄露。

祖尼人有很多保护这些宗教圣物和仪式不为人所知的方法。例如，部落禁止透过房间窗户偷看室内，特别是在夜晚。1890 年，有两个人在晚上透过窗户偷看被当作巫婆受到审判和鞭打。即便是现在，很多祖尼人的房子都设有夜间监视的户外照明，门口也有警犬防范入侵者。在进行宗教仪式的过程中，房子内外都有人把守，同时协助保密的还有坚实的墙壁。此外，祖尼人对禁忌的一贯尊重和平时良好的礼仪习惯都有助于保护祖尼村落的隐私和秘密。

你怎么看?

1. 对祖尼人来说隐私或保密的内容是什么？
2. 祖尼人要保护这些隐私和秘密的内容不被哪些人知道？
3. 祖尼人如何用行动来保护这些隐私内容，即保护与这些事情相关的隐私？
4. 你认为祖尼人为什么要努力保护与这些事情相关的隐私？

重点思考练习

找出隐私行为之间的差异之处

仔细阅读下面的材料，找出作者所描述的不同社会和不同时代的人们在隐私行为方面的差异之处。然后回答"你怎么看？"这一部分的问题，准备与全班讨论你的答案。

The Right to Privacy Is a Myth

by Bruno Bettelheim

from **The Saturday Evening Post**, July 7, 1968

Everywhere one turns these days it seems that the right to privacy is constantly under assault. If one is not being assailed by gratuitous noise and information, then some company or government agency is asking indiscreet questions, probing for innermost feelings. Is nothing private any more, nothing sacred to the individual? Can't people live their own lives, be left alone to be themselves in this country? Don't we all resent these intrusions? Then why do we permit such disregard for our privacy?

I was pondering these questions one night recently, in solitude, behind the closed doors of my room As I began to write these thoughts down, my eyes strayed to the picture I had hung on the wall over my desk, and I had to laugh at myself. There I had put a copy of a Breughel painting, teeming with people and life. The figures in the painting were going about their business, and doing it, apparently, with all the more gusto because they were in the presence of others. They didn't seem to want or need privacy. Why was this? Is our passion for privacy just a recent, temporary phenomenon, destined soon to die away?

When I studied as a youngster, the door to my room had to be closed, and everything had to be quiet. Only then could I concentrate on myself and my work to the exclusion of everything else. But my own children study best with the door open and the record player going full blast, and in this radically different setting they learn as much and as well as I did. Why, then, do I still need privacy, and why do they not seem to need it?

《隐私权只是一个神话》

撰稿：布鲁诺·贝特尔海姆

1968 年 7 月 7 日《星期六晚报》

最近个人隐私似乎在哪儿都轮番遭到攻击。一个人要么就是被无端的噪音和讯息所困扰，要么就是一些公司或政府机构提出一些轻率的问题，探究人们最内心的感受。对个人来说，不再有任何隐私、不再有任何神圣的事情了吗？在这个国家，人们不能有自己的生活，不能被单独留下来吗？我们难道不是都憎恨这些干扰吗？为什么我们又会容许这些无视我们隐私的行为呢？

这两天晚上我一个人在家，紧闭着我的房门，思考了这些问题。当我开始把这些想法写下来的时候，我的眼睛被正对桌子那面墙上的一幅画给吸引住了。我忍不住开始嘲笑我自己。那是我挂在墙上的一幅勃鲁盖尔画作的复制品，画里充满了各种人和生活的元素：人们在四处忙碌做生意，他们在人前显得是那样热情积极，看上去似乎不想要或者不需要任何隐私。为什么会这样呢？难道我们对隐私的热情是最近才发生的短暂现象，并且注定即将消失吗？

在我还在上学念书的青少年时期，我关着房门，一切都是那样安静。只有这样我才能集中精力、排除一切杂念，专注于自己和我的工作。相反，我的孩子在读书的时候喜欢把门打开，把录音机开到最大声。在这样两种截然不同的环境里，他们学到的东西和我的一样多。那么为什么我还需要隐私，为什么他们看起来并不需要它？

Maybe the answer is that we all function best when in closest communion with what seems (to us) to symbolize our highest values I, growing up before the age of mass culture, had to create for myself a setting that emphasized personal uniqueness and individual development before I could concentrate on a learning task designed (whether I knew it or not) to achieve a high degree of individuality. My children, for the same reason, need to emphasize communality as they work. The music of the Beatles reassures them, just as my studying in privacy reassured me. It gives them the feeling that even when alone at their studies they are still in touch with what counts most in their lives: a sense of connection with their age group. How fast the attitude toward privacy can change, I thought.....

My Victorian parents, when they went out to dinner, preferred a spacious restaurant with their table set off by ample distance from the next one. Nowadays young people prefer to crowd together in small discotheques, and the hippies think nothing of sleeping many to a room....

Historically, privacy has always been a luxury few could afford. One need not go far back to a time when whole families lived together in one room. Nobody had privacy then. One could not hide skeletons in the closet, because there were no closets. In colonial days, even among the affluent, a family had to be quite well off to afford separate bedrooms, one for the parents and one for all the children....

Lewis Mumford writes that the first radical change, which was to alter the form of the medieval house, was the development of a sense of privacy. This meant, in effect, withdrawal at will from the common life and the common interest of one's fellows. Privacy in sleep, privacy in eating, privacy in religious and social rituals, finally privacy in thought.... In the castles of the 13th Century, one notes the existence of a private bedroom for the noble owners... Privacy in bed came first in Italy among the upper classes only....

This wish for privacy is closely connected with the increased value placed on private property. My home is my castle, where I am protected from anyone's intruding on my privacy. It was the lord of the castle who first claimed privacy for himself. Whoever owns no place of his own, owns no privacy either.

也许答案在于，只有在与那些（对我们来说）似乎象征着最高价值的东西进行最亲密的交流时，我们才能全心投入、思维全速运转。我成长在大众文化出现的年代之前，这使我不得不为自己创造出一种强调个人独特性和个人发展的环境，只有这样我才能集中精力在某项学习任务上，而这项任务是为了实现更高程度的自我个性而设计的（不管事先我是否了解它）。出于相同的原因，我的孩子们在工作的时候却要强调合作和团结。甲壳虫乐队的音乐让他们安心，这和我一个人学习时的私密环境给我的感受一样。音乐给予了他们一种即便是独自学习，也仍然保持着与同龄人相连接的感觉，这对他们的生活来说至关重要。人们对隐私态度的转变究竟有多快，这引发了我的思考……

我的父母生活在维多利亚时代，当他们出去吃晚饭时，喜欢找一家宽敞的餐厅，能让他们与邻桌之间保持足够的距离。而现在的年轻人喜欢一群人聚在一起，去小迪斯科舞厅，嬉皮士们则更愿意一堆人挤在一个房间里睡觉……

历史上，隐私一直是少数人才能享受的奢侈品。一个大家庭住在一个房间的时代离我们并不久远。那时没有人有隐私。人们不能在柜子里藏骷髅，因为家里没有橱柜。在殖民地时代，即便是富人，家庭的经济条件也必须足够宽裕也才能负担起有两间独立卧室的房子：一间给父母，剩下一间给所有的孩子……

刘易斯·芒福德写道，隐私意识的发展导致了中世纪房屋结构的第一次彻底变革。实际上这意味着，人们可以任意退出与同伴的共同生活和共同利益。在睡眠、饮食、宗教和社会仪式上的隐私，最终发展到思想上的隐私……历史记载，13世纪的城堡里开始出现了贵族领主的私人卧室……床第的隐私最早出现在意大利，只有上层阶级才拥有……

这种对隐私的渴求是与越来越重视私有财产的价值观紧密联系在一起的。"我的家就是我的城堡，在那里可以保护我免受任何人侵犯我的隐私。"如此一来，城堡的主人率先宣告了自己的隐私权。没有属于自己的土地的人，也没有隐私。

The more class-structured a society becomes, the more privacy do its privileged members demand. How understandable, then, that a society which tries to do away with class structure should also try to do away with privacy, and demand that ever-larger areas of life should be public.

What is harder to realize is that as long as everyone knows everything about everyone else, there is no need for informers, for elaborate spy systems, for bugging, in order to know what people do, say and think. Witness the absence of crime, delinquency and other antisocial behavior in the Israeli agricultural communal settlements, the kibbutzim. They have no police because there is no need for policing. This is because everyone there lives much more collectively and openly than we do here Personally, I felt suffocated by the lack of privacy when I visited a kibbutz. But I could not blind myself to the incredibly successful control of antisocial behavior in this society.

Among the unresolved problems of modem city life is the prevalence of fear in our streets. Perhaps here the solution has nothing to do with reconstructing our cities, or an endless enlarging of the police forces within them. What we need, in my opinion, is a return to much smaller, more self-contained communities

 In what way might ideas of privacy be related to an absence of crime and other antisocial behavior on this Israeli kibbutz?   ☞

社会的阶级结构越来越多，与此同时它的特权阶层也需要更多的隐私。那么也就不难理解，如果一个社会要试图废除阶级结构，就要同时取消隐私权，并要求开放比以往更广泛的生活领域。

但这是很难实现的，只要每个人都了解任何其他人的所有事情，那就不用为了掌握人们的行动、话语和思考而需要线人告密了，也就更不需要设计精妙的间谍系统和窃听工具了。在以色列的农业合作聚居区——基布兹（集体农场），这里没有犯罪、没有行为不端和其他反社会行为；没有警察，因为没有任何维护治安的需要。每个人的生活都比我们国家的更集体化、更公开化。在探访基布兹的时候，由于缺乏隐私，我个人感到非常窒息，但这个地方令人难以置信地成功控制了反社会行为的成就，令我无法视而不见。

现代城市生活中有许多未能解决的问题，其中一种是我们的大街上普遍存在的恐惧。重建我们的城市、或无休止地扩充警力都不是很有效的解决方案。在我看来，我们需要的是回归到更小、更独立自足的社区生活，在这样的社区里现在有很多私密的事情都可以公开，我们也能更多地与他人分享，也更了解彼此。

在以色列的基布兹地区，隐私的观念与无犯罪、无其他反社会行为的情况是以何种方式相关联的？

where a great deal of what is now private can become public; where we would share more and know much more about each other.

Where does all this leave me? Despite all of my realizations, I do not cherish privacy less, and I still resent deeply any intrusion upon it...

Neither a medieval absence of privacy nor a Big Brother's spying that leaves nothing unpublic will do. What we must strive for, as is true of most important human questions, is the right balance between what should be respected as private in our lives and what belongs to our more-or-less public and communal life. Then our lives will be neither fortified castles nor public places.

What do you think?

1. What differences in privacy behavior does the author describe between his generation and his children's generation? Between his parent's generation and his children's generation?

2. What does the author tell us about the historical development of privacy? What do you think might be the costs and benefits of a medieval absence of privacy?

3. What does the author tell us about privacy behavior on an Israeli kibbutz? How do his observations lead him to suggest a solution for the unresolved problems of modern city life?

4. How do your attitudes about privacy compare with the author's? What do you think is the right balance between the public and private parts of our lives?

　　有没有可能，现在所有这一切都会离我而去？那时，除去我所有的财产，我不会减少一丝一毫对隐私的珍视，我仍然会深深地厌恶任何对隐私的侵犯……

　　现在既不是缺乏隐私的中世纪，也没有哪个"老大哥"的监视导致我们什么秘密的事情都没法做。和许多最重要的人类问题一样真实的是，在某些应当被尊重的隐私，和属于多少有些公共和集体的生活之间，我们必须争取找到一种正确的平衡。

你怎么看?

1. 上文中，作者所描述的他这一代人和他的子女一代在隐私行为上有哪些不同？他的父母一代和他的子女一代之间有什么不同？

2. 有关隐私的历史发展，作者告诉了我们什么？你觉得中世纪由于缺少隐私会产生哪些利弊得失？

3. 关于以色列的基布兹集体农业定居区，作者告诉了我们什么？他对基布兹的考察促使他对解决现代城市生活中悬而未决的问题提出了什么建议？

4. 如何比较你和作者对于隐私的态度和看法？你认为在我们的生活中公共和私人部分之间正确的平衡应当是什么？

Using the Lesson

1.Imagine that you are working for an architectural firm. Design a house in which you would like to live. Then explain how the house you have designed reflects your ideas about the need for privacy.

2.Gulliver's Travels is a famous book written by Jonathan Swift. It contains descriptions of several imaginary cultures and presents examples of the privacy behavior of the people who live in them. Read this book and compare the privacy behavior of the people in two of the cultures. Then report your findings to the rest of the class.

3.Write a story about a person living in the United States who wants to keep something private. In your story, describe what the person wants to keep private and what you think are the reasons for the person's privacy behavior.

4.In your privacy journal, write at least three questions you have about privacy.

知识运用

1. 假设你在一家建筑公司工作，设计一幢你想要住的房子，然后说明你设计的这幢房子如何反映出你对隐私需求的想法。

2. 乔纳森·斯威夫特的著名小说《格列佛游记》中描述了几种假想的社会文化，并列举了生活在这些文化环境中的人们的一些隐私行为。阅读这本书，从中选出并比较其中两种文化环境中人们的隐私行为，然后向全班其他同学报告你的发现。

3. 写一个故事，描述一个生活在美国并希望保护某些隐私的人。在你的故事中描述这个人想要保护的隐私是什么，并说明这个人隐私行为的原因。

4. 在关于隐私的笔记里，写下至少三个有关隐私的问题。

Unit Three
What Are Some Benefits and Costs of Privacy?

Purpose of Unit

Maintaining privacy entails certain consequences. Some consequences are benefits, or advantages; some are costs, or disadvantages. It is important to recognize and consider the consequences of privacy in making decisions about issues of privacy. If you are trying to decide in a particular situation whether to recognize a claim to privacy, you need to think about what the benefits and costs might be of maintaining privacy in that situation.

In this unit, you will identify some common benefits and costs of privacy, and you will explore the consequences of privacy in a number of specific situations. As you will see, different individuals may have different opinions about whether the right to privacy should be protected in a particular situation.

第三单元：隐私会产生哪些利弊得失？

单元目标

　　保护隐私会产生某些结果，其中有些结果是利处（或优点），有些则是弊处（或缺点）。在决定隐私问题时，认识和考虑隐私的结果是非常重要的。如果你们要在某种特定情况下决定是否应当认可某种对隐私的要求，就需要考虑在那样的情况下保护隐私会有哪些利弊得失。

　　在本单元中，你们会认识隐私的某些常见的利弊得失，你们也将在许多特定的情况中探寻隐私的结果。正如你们将发现的，对某种特定情况下是否需要保护隐私权，每个人都有不同的看法。

 What benefits and costs of privacy are illustrated by these photographs?

这些照片表现了隐私的哪些利弊得失？

LESSON 6
What Are the Possible Consequences of Privacy?

Purpose of Lesson

In this lesson you examine some of the possible consequences of privacy and classify them as benefits or costs. You also evaluate positions on issues of privacy by thinking about the consequences of privacy. When you have completed this lesson, you should be able to explain some common benefits and costs of privacy.

Terms to Know

writs of assistance   conformity   totalitarian

creativity   intellectual stimulation

Critical Thinking Exercise

EXAMINING CONSEQUENCES OF PRIVACY

Your teacher will divide your class into small groups. Each group should read the situations below, list the possible consequences of privacy in each situation, and classify these consequences as benefits-advantages or as costs-disadvantages. Each group should be prepared to share its lists of benefits and costs with the class.

1. Before the American Revolution, English officials in the colonies used general search warrants, called writs of assistance, to enter the colonists' homes at any time and search them for evidence of crimes. Now, because of the Fourth Amendment to the U.S. Constitution, government officials cannot use general search warrants to search for evidence of crimes. Instead, they can only get a warrant if they first convince a judge that there is good reason to believe specific evidence of a crime will be found in a particular place. Then, if the judge is convinced, he or she issues a specific search warrant particularly describing the place to be searched and the persons or things to be seized.

第六课：隐私会产生哪些结果？

本课目标

在本课中，你们将研究隐私可能产生的结果，并将它们分为利益（或好处）和弊处（或损失）这两类。你们也要通过思考隐私的结果，来评估针对不同的隐私问题的不同观点。学完本课后，你们应当能够解释保护隐私通常导致的利弊得失。

掌握词汇

协查令　　　一致性　　　极权主义
创造力　　　智力刺激

重点思考练习

研究隐私的结果

老师会把你们班分成若干小组。每个小组应阅读以下材料，找出每段文字中描述的隐私可能产生的结果，并将这些结果分为利益（或优点）或损失（缺点）。各组应当准备与全班分享自己列出的利弊得失。

1. 美国独立战争前，殖民地的英国官员通常使用一种叫做"协查令"的一般搜查令，这样他们可以随时进入殖民地居民的家中，搜寻他们的犯罪证据。现在，基于美国联邦宪法第四修正案，政府官员不能使用一般搜查令搜寻犯罪证据。相反，除非他们首先有充分理由说服法官，使法官相信在某个特定地点可以找到特定的犯罪证据，否则他们无法得到法官的批准和授权。如果法官被说服了，他或她将颁布一种专门搜查令，具体描述要被搜查的地方和要被扣押的人或物。

2.Psychiatrists, psychologists, and other counselors keep records and notes of their sessions with patients and clients. These records and notes are highly confidential, and may not be disclosed to anyone under most circumstances.

3. Under most circumstances, a lawyer may not reveal what a client has said to him or her in private.

4. When Shandra's brother told her he had AIDS, she cried and cried at home. But Shandra never let her feelings show at school. When Shandra's friends asked her what was bothering her, she just shook her head.

As you can see, some consequences of privacy are benefits and some are costs. The next two sections describe some of the most common benefits and costs of privacy. As you read these sections, think about the benefits and costs that result from privacy in your life.

 How did the Fourth Amendment curtail the English practice of using writs of assistance to search colonial homes and businesses? ☞

第四修正案如何限制了英国官员使用协查令搜查殖民地家庭和企业的做法？

2. 精神病医师、心理学家和其他心理顾问会保存他们与病人或当事人的谈话记录和笔记。这些记录和笔记是高度机密的，在大多数情况下不得向任何人披露。

3. 在大多数情况下，律师不得公开当事人私下与他或她交谈的内容。

4. 当尚德拉的哥哥告诉她他患有艾滋病时，她在家里一直哭。但是她从来没有在学校表露过她的感受。当尚德拉的朋友问她有什么困扰时，她只是摇了摇头。

　　正如以上你们所读到的，有些隐私的结果是利益，而有些结果则是损失。以下两段会描述隐私最常见的利弊得失。阅读下文，思考在你们的生活中隐私带来的利弊得失。

What are the benefits of privacy?

FREEDOM, Privacy helps people think and act freely, without unreasonable influence or control by others. This freedom may prevent a society from becoming totalitarian, that is, subject to complete control by a dictator or ruling party.

Example: In private places where they cannot be overheard, people may feel free to speak with their family and friends about ideas and beliefs that may not be popular with others.

SECURITY. Respect for privacy fosters a sense of security; if one's privacy is respected, one can feel safe and secure.

Example: If your family and friends respect your privacy, you can feel secure that they will not bother you when you want to be alone or embarrass you by revealing things you want to keep private.

INDIVIDUALITY. Without privacy, the pressure to be like others might inhibit an individual from forming his or her own values, beliefs, and opinions.

Example: Sometimes families, gangs, and whole societies do not allow their members to have much privacy. In these circumstances people often feel they have to go along with whatever the group or its leaders consider to be correct beliefs and behavior.

How were freedom, security, and individuality undermined in Nazi Germany by the absence of privacy? ☞

什么是隐私的利益?

　　自由：保护隐私有助于人们自由地思考和行动，不受他人不合理的影响或控制。这种自由可以让一个社会避免沦为极权主义，即彻底受某个独裁者或执政党控制的社会。

　　例如：在无法被偷听到的私密场所，人们可以非常自由地对家人和朋友说出自己的看法和信仰，也许这些看法和信仰并不受其他人欢迎。

　　安全：人们对隐私的尊重形成了一种安全感；如果一个人的隐私得到尊重，他或她会感到安全和放心。

　　例如：如果你的家人和朋友尊重你的隐私，你会很安心，相信他们不会在你想要一个人独处的时候打扰你，或是泄露你想要保密的事情让你难堪。

　　个性：如果没有隐私，就会面临要与他人一致的压力，这可能会使一个人无法形成他或她自己的价值观、信仰和观点。

　　例如：有时候，家庭、团体和整个社会不允许其成员保有很多隐私。在这种情况下人们通常会觉得，必须要赞同和跟随团体及其领导人认为是正确的信仰和行动。

在纳粹德国缺乏隐私的情况下，自由、安全和个性是如何被破坏的？

PROTECTION OF ECONOMIC INTERESTS. Privacy enables people to keep their ideas, plans, and inventions secret. This may help them create and sell new products and compete with others.

Example: Suppose you designed a T-shirt that you thought would sell well and make a lot of money. Keeping your idea secret until you created the T-shirts and had them ready to sell would prevent others from taking your idea.

CREATIVITY. Privacy may be necessary for creative thought or work.

Example: Suppose you were painting a picture and someone was looking over your shoulder as you painted. You might feel as though that person was judging you, or worry about what the person would think of your painting. Or suppose people were talking near you or asking you questions. You might find it difficult to concentrate.

INTIMACY. Privacy is necessary for people to develop warm and affectionate relationships with other people.

Example: Suppose there was no place you could go to be alone with someone or there was no way to communicate in private. You might not be willing to express your innermost thoughts and feelings and you might find it difficult to develop close relationships with anyone.

Critical Thinking Exercise

IDENTIFYING AND DESCRIBING THE BENEFITS OF PRIVACY

Work with a study partner to answer the following questions. Include examples to explain or illustrate your ideas.

1. Do you think privacy is truly essential for people to develop close relationships? Why or why not?

2. What pressures to be like other people exist in your school and community? In what way does having privacy free you from those pressures and enable you to develop your own thoughts, feelings, and lifestyle?

3. How would you feel if no one respected the privacy of your personal possessions or if people did not respect your wishes when you wanted to be alone?

4. In what ways docs privacy help you to be creative?

保护经济利益：隐私使人们能够将自己的想法、计划和发明得以保密。这可能会有助于创造和销售新产品，并与他人竞争。

例如：假设你设计出一款 T 恤，并觉得这件衣服会很畅销并能赚很多钱，那么你就要将这个想法保密，直到 T 恤制作完成并准备出售为止，这样才能防止别人剽窃你的创意。

创意：隐私对创造性思维或工作来说是必要的。

例如：假设你画了一幅画，有人站在你背后看你作画，你可能会觉得这个人是在判断你，或是担心这个人会怎么看待你的作品。又或者假使你画画的时候，一直有人在你周围说话或是问你问题，你可能会很难集中精力。

亲密：隐私对人们与他人建立热情和友好的关系是必要的。

例如：假设你找不到一个可以跟某人单独相处的地方，或是缺乏与某人私下交流的方式，你会不愿意表达自己内心的想法和感受，并发现很难与任何人建立亲密关系。

重点思考练习

识别和描述隐私的利益

与一位同学一起合作回答下列问题，回答时请举例解释或说明你们的想法。

1. 你认为隐私对人们之间建立亲密关系是真正必需的吗？为什么？为什么不？

2. 在你的学校和社区里，是否存在着必须与他人保持一致的压力？这些压力是什么？拥有隐私使你在哪些方面从这种压力中释放出来，并建立起自己的想法、感受和生活方式？

3. 如果没有人尊重你的个人隐私或财产，你会感觉如何？或者，如果人们不尊重你的意愿，你想一个人独处的时候，你会感觉如何？

4. 隐私在哪些方面帮助你变得富有创意？

What are the costs of privacy?

LONELINESS AND ALIENATION. Too much privacy can lead to loneliness and to poor relations with others.

Example: Suppose a person always kept his or her feelings private. Others might be reluctant to share their feelings with someone who never reciprocates. With no one to talk to, the person might feel cut off and lonely.

LOSS OF STIMULATION AND INTELLECTUAL GROWTH. People correct errors in their thinking and learn new ideas through interaction with other people; too much privacy can inhibit the exchange of ideas and prevent learning from others.

Example: Some people are afraid to express their views for fear of being ridiculed. Because they keep their thoughts to themselves, it is difficult for them to become aware of errors and refine their thinking. Also, other people never benefit from their ideas.

MISBEHAVIOR AND LAWLESSNESS. Privacy enables unlawful behavior to remain undiscovered and unpunished.

Example: By acting in private, without being observed, people can plan and commit crimes and hide evidence of their crimes.

FINANCIAL COSTS. Maintaining privacy increases the cost of doing things.

Example: A company has to spend more to provide separate offices for its employees than to have them all work in a single large room.

LACK OF ACCOUNTABILITY. Privacy enables people to do things that others cannot observe; as a result, it may be impossible to hold them responsible for wrongdoing.

Example: Without supervision, people might take shortcuts in their work, cheat on a test, or steal. Other people might never discover what has been done or there may be no way to prove who is responsible.

什么是隐私的损失？

孤独和疏远：过多的隐私会导致孤独感，并与他人关系不佳。例如：假设一个人始终将自己的感受保密，而对于那些从不与他人交换感受的人，人们也不愿意与他们分享心情，因此这个人始终无法找到倾诉对象，就会感到孤独和被疏远。

缺乏激励和知识增长的损失：人们通过他人的交流，来纠正自己想法上的错误，并学习新的观念；过多的隐私会阻止和妨碍人们之间观念的交流，使人们无法向他人学习。

例如：有些人因为怕被人嘲笑而不敢表达自己的观点，并将自己的想法隐藏起来，因此他们很难意识到自己想法中的错误并加以改善。同时，其他人也永远无法从他们的想法中获益。

品行不端和目无法纪：隐私使非法行为不被发现，犯罪的人逃脱惩罚。

例如：通过不被发现的秘密行动，人们可以计划和实施犯罪，并隐藏其犯罪证据。

经济损失：保护隐私增加了做某些事情的成本。

例如：比起让员工们都挤在一间大房子里，公司必须花更多钱为员工提供单独的办公室。

缺乏责任感：隐私使人们能够做某些事而不被其他人发现，这样一来，就无法追究当事人做错事的责任了。

例如：没有监督，人们可能会在工作中投机取巧、在考试中作弊或偷窃。这些事情可能永远不会被人发现，或者永远也无法证明谁应当为此事负责。

Critical Thinking Exercise

IDENTIFYING AND DESCRIBING THE COSTS OF PRIVACY

Work with a study partner to answer the following questions. Include examples to explain or illustrate your ideas.

1. Could too much privacy inhibit your ability to be creative? Explain your answer.

2. How might too much privacy cause a person to have problems in developing friendships or in relating to other people?

3. How can maintaining privacy increase the cost of doing things?

4. Do you think privacy makes it possible for people to commit crimes and not get caught? Why or why not?

5. Do you think privacy makes it more difficult to hold people responsible for their actions? Why or why not?

Using the Lesson

1. Identify an issue of privacy in the news media or make up an example. Prepare a chart that lists the consequences of maintaining privacy in the situation and identify these consequences as benefits or costs. Be prepared to explain the issue to your class.

2. Working with your teacher, invite a law enforcement officer or an attorney to class to discuss his or her ideas about the benefits and costs of privacy. Prepare list of questions to ask.

重点思考练习

识别和描述隐私的损失

与一位同学一起合作回答下列问题。回答时请举例解释或说明你们的想法。

1. 过多的隐私会不会妨碍你的创意能力？解释你的答案。

2. 在人们与他人建立友谊或发展人际关系时，过多的隐私会怎样带来一些问题？

3. 保护隐私如何增加了做事情的成本？

4. 你是否认为隐私可能让人们犯下罪行却并不被发现？为什么？为什么不？

5. 你是否认为隐私使人们更难为自己的行为负责？为什么？为什么不？

知识运用

1. 在新闻媒体的报道中找出一个有关隐私的问题，或者自己编写一个案例。准备一个表格，列出在这个案例中保护隐私的结果，并说明哪些结果是利益，哪些是损失。准备向全班解释你的案例和观点。

2. 与老师一起邀请一位执法人员或律师到班上来，和大家讨论他或她对保护隐私的利弊得失的看法。准备好你们要对嘉宾提出的问题。

LESSON 7

What Might Be Some of the Benefits and Costs of Confidentiality?

Purpose of Lesson

This lesson provides an opportunity to identify the benefits and costs of privacy in a specific situation, and to evaluate the importance of these benefits and costs. This lesson also provides an opportunity to role-play an administrative hearing concerning the privacy obligations of lawyers and therapists.

When you have completed this lesson, you should be able to identify benefits and costs and use these ideas to evaluate, take, and defend positions on issues of privacy.

Term to Know

hearsay

Why is it important to evaluate the benefits and costs of privacy?

Evaluating the benefits and costs of privacy is important before making decisions about issues of privacy. We need to decide which consequences of privacy are most important to us. Are the benefits more important than the costs? Or do we think the costs outweigh the benefits?

People may disagree about which benefits and costs of protecting privacy in a particular situation are most important. For example, consider a rule that protects the privacy of student lockers. Everyone would agree that the benefits of this rule include protection of the students' right to privacy and protection of their personal property. Everyone would also agree that the costs of this rule include interference with the school administrators' ability to find illegal drugs, weapons, or other improper things that might be hidden in lockers.

Some people might think that the benefits of this rule protecting the students' right to privacy outweigh its costs. Others might think that the costs outweigh the benefits. As you can see, it is important to consider benefits and costs when examining issues regarding privacy.

第七课：隐私会产生哪些利弊得失？

本课目标

本课中，你们将有机会在特定情境中找出隐私的利弊得失，并权衡这些利弊得失的重要性。你们也将有机会进行一次角色扮演，参与一场关于律师和医生隐私规定的模拟行政听证会。

学完本课后，你们应当能够识别隐私的利弊得失，并运用这些观念来评估、选择和论证有关隐私问题的各种观点。

掌握词汇

谣言

评估隐私的利弊得失为什么是重要的？

对有关隐私问题做决定之前，评估隐私的利弊得失是很重要的。我们需要决定隐私的哪些结果对我们来说是最重要的，是利大于弊？还是弊大于利？

在某种特定情况下保护隐私的利弊得失中，人们对哪种结果更重要的意见不一。譬如，试想想某个保护学生储物柜隐私的规定，每个人都会同意，这项规定的利益包括：保护了学生的隐私权，保护了学生的个人财产；每个人也会同意，这项规定的损失包括：干扰和影响学校管理人员发现学生在储物柜中藏匿非法毒品、武器或其他不当物品的能力。

针对该项保护学生隐私权的规定，有些人可能会认为利大于弊。而其他人可能会认为弊大于利。正如你们所看到的，在研究有关隐私的问题之前，首先考虑利弊得失是很重要的。

Critical Thinking Exercise

EXPLAINING SOME CONSEQUENCES OF CONFIDENTIALITY

Work in study groups to complete this exercise. As you read the following adaptation of a newspaper article, think about the consequences of requiring lawyers and therapists to keep their clients' confessions confidential. Then complete the tasks and answer the questions that have been assigned to your group in the section "Identifying Benefits and Costs." Be prepared to share your answers with the class.

A Fine Line: To Tell or Not to Tell

By Barry Siegel Times Staff Writer

Los Angeles Times

Wednesday December 29,1993

Leroy Phillips, Jr. is a criminal defense attorney in Chattanooga, Tennessee. He had always believed that the rules for being a defense attorney were very clear: you never shared your client's confidences with anyone, never gave an inch to the prosecutor, were a strong adversary of the state and an even stronger advocate of the defendant. The confidentiality privilege is a sacrosanct basis for how lawyers work. People must know they can tell their lawyer anything and it won't be divulged. Then in May, 1993, Phillips received a phone call that called his beliefs into question.

In response to the call, Phillips met the caller-an unassuming, rather awkward young man dressed in plain work clothes-who confessed to an unsolved homicide. "I did it," Phil Payne told Phillips. "I killed that store clerk last night. I thought she was my ex-girlfriend." At that point, attorney Phillips was faced with a difficult moral and legal dilemma. When an attorney is admitted to the bar, he takes an oath to keep his clients' confessions confidential. In Tennessee, a legal obligation exists as well; to divulge a client's confidence is a felony that carries a possible five-year prison term. Only if a client directly threatens to kill someone does the law oblige the attorney to inform authorities. Phil Payne never directly threatened to kill anyone; only by implication did he suggest that he might kill again. What was the lawyer to do?

重点思考练习

说明隐私的某些结果

　　分成小组来完成本次练习。在阅读下文的报纸摘录时，思考律师和医师需要对其当事人的供词和口述保密的结果。完成本练习并回答"识别隐私的利弊得失"部分中分配给你们小组的问题。准备与全班分享你们的答案。

《一线之隔：说或不说》

撰稿：巴里·西格尔

1993 年 12 月 29 日星期三《洛杉矶时报》

　　勒罗伊·菲利普斯是田纳西州查塔努加的一位刑事辩护律师。他始终认为，作为一个辩护律师应当有明确的准则，那就是：永远不与任何人分享你的当事人的机密，永远不能让原告得寸进尺；既要做其他辩护律师最强劲的对手，更是被告最有力的辩护人。律师工作中神圣不可侵犯的基础是保密特权。人们必须确保他们可以跟自己的律师说任何话，并且不会被泄露。然而在 1993 年 5 月，菲利普斯接到的一个电话挑战了他的信仰。

　　在接电话的时候，菲利普会见了这个打电话的人——一个谦逊而笨拙、穿着朴素工作服的青年男人——他坦承自己谋杀未遂。"是我干的，"菲尔·佩恩告诉菲利普斯："昨晚我杀了那家商店的店员。我以为她是我的前女友。"此时，律师菲利普斯面临着棘手的道德和法律困境。在被授予律师资格时，他曾经发誓对自己当事人的供词保密。在田纳西州，这项法律也同样适用：泄露当事人的秘密是一项重罪，可能要被判 5 年徒刑。只有在当事人直接威胁要杀死某人时，法律才会要求律师告知当局。菲尔·佩恩没有直接威胁要杀死任何人，只是暗示他可能会再次行凶，那么这位律师该怎么办？

Here is Phil Payne's story. Two weeks earlier, Payne had tried to visit a former girlfriend whom he had dated nine years before. The girl, however, ran him off. Distraught, Payne went to a bar and drank beer all evening, after which he went back to the girl's house planning to kill her. When she failed to answer the door, Payne began driving around, oblivious to his whereabouts. He finally stopped for cigarettes at an all-night market where he saw a female clerk making coffee. When Payne saw the clerk, he thought of his ex-girlfriend who had always fixed coffee for him; in his mind, he "saw" the girlfriend, not an unknown clerk. He pulled out a gun, shot the clerk and drove back to his mother's home where he went to bed.

The attorney asked, "What do you want me to do?" Payne, smiling, said "I know I did a terrible thing and I don't want to harm anyone else. I need to be punished but I want help, too." This request put Phillips in a quandary. If he turned Payne over to the police and Payne subsequently confessed, the young man would go to jail. Payne, however, did not appear to understand his rights, and Phillips was morally and legally obliged to explain the rights and the consequences if he turned himself in. The attorney therefore said, "If you go to the police, they might put you in a jail cell for the rest of your life. If you go through me, they might put you in a hospital. If you are mentally ill, you have a right to be treated. Do you want that?" "Yes, yes I do."

What rights of privacy should be extended to persons suspected of violating the law?   ☞

　　现在来说说菲尔·佩恩的故事。两个星期前，佩恩曾试图寻找9年前跟他谈过恋爱的前女友，但这个女孩儿从他手上逃跑了。佩恩气得发狂，于是跑到一家酒吧喝了一整晚啤酒，然后又回到前女友家，打算要杀死她。但她没来应门，佩恩开始漫无目的开着车乱转。后来他把车停在一家24小时商店的门口，打算进去买包烟。在店里他看到一个女店员正在煮咖啡，佩恩想起他的前女友以前也总为他冲咖啡，他以为自己"看到"了前女友（而不是这位陌生的女店员）。随后他掏出枪，对着女店员开了一枪，然后开车回到他母亲的家中睡下了。

　　律师问他："你想要我怎么做？"佩恩微笑着说："我知道我做了可怕的事情，我不想伤害任何其他人。我会受到惩罚，但我也需要帮助。"佩恩的要求令菲利普斯左右为难。如果他把佩恩交给警察，佩恩随后对自己的罪行供认不讳，这个年轻人就会坐牢。然而佩恩似乎并不了解自己所拥有的权利，菲利普斯在道德和法律上都有义务向他解释这些权利，以及向佩恩说明如果他去自首将会有什么后果。因此律师对佩恩说："如果你去警察局，他们可能让你的余生都在监狱里度过。如果你是精神病患者，你就有权获得治疗。你想要这样做吗？""是的，我想。"

什么隐私权应扩展到犯罪嫌疑人？

Phillips paid a visit to assistant district attorney Stan Lanzo. He told Lanzo the story of this delusional man who had admitted to murder but who seemed to be totally insane. Phillips said, "1 am worried about the girlfriend but he hasn't said he plans to kill her so I cannot legally turn him in." Lanzo listened as Phillips suggested that they file a petition, put Payne in a hospital and examine him. His client would be off the street and whatever he said to the doctor would be usable only on the sanity issue and not on the question of guilt. Now Lanzo faced a dilemma as well. Phillips was a lawyer, not a psychologist. As a district attorney he couldn't commit Payne on the strength of a lawyer's analysis alone.

Phillips felt increasing concern about the ex-girlfriend who was in danger with Payne still at large. If he shared Payne's secrets, however, he could be reprimanded by the Tennessee Bar Association and perhaps even sued Phillips turned to George Bercaw, a clinical psychologist, who administered a battery of tests. After a period of weeks, Bercaw encouraged the attorney to resolve the matter with the prosecutors although he was not too worried at that point.

In July 1993, Bercaw received a call from Payne's mother who reported that Payne had disappeared. Bercaw contacted Phillips, Phillips' first thought was to contact the ex-girlfriend. His second thought was, how could he? He'd be violating his trust with his client. Phillips' phone rang an hour later. It was Payne who explained that he had spent most of the time driving around his girlfriend's house and in a cemetery talking with the girl's dead mother and listening to voices from the grave. The psychologist realized that Payne was indeed dangerous and might kill or commit suicide Bercaw decided that moral obligations should take precedence over legal ones, especially after Payne's mother said that he talked of killing both the girlfriend and himself. Bercaw relayed this information to Phillips saying, "Leroy, I know you have an obligation as a lawyer, but I believe the law permits me to do more. The law says if I feel he's dangerous to himself or others, I can report him."

Phillips spoke to his client: "Mr. Bercaw thinks you're very ill. He believes that you need help and should turn yourself in. They will put you in jail, but eventually you will be examined to see if you should be put in a hospital." When Payne agreed, Phillips admonished him to talk only to the doctors, not the police.

菲利普斯拜访了地区助理检察官斯坦·兰佐。他告诉兰佐,有个妄想症的男人承认自己杀了人,但这个人似乎完全是个疯子。菲利普斯说:"我很担心他说的那个女孩(佩恩的前女友),但他没有跟我说他计划杀死她,我不能依法举报他。"菲利普斯向兰佐建议,由地方法院提起诉讼,将佩恩送到医院去做检查。这样一来他的这位当事人就不会流窜在外,他跟医生说的所有话将只适用于神智清醒的状况,而不会用在问罪上。现在轮到兰佐也面临两难局面了。菲利普斯是一名律师,而不是一个心理医师。作为一个地方检察官,他不能单凭一个律师的分析就把佩恩送上法庭。

菲利普斯越来越担心仍然处于佩恩威胁之下的那位女孩。但如果他暴露了佩恩的秘密,他会受到田纳西州律师协会的谴责甚至是被起诉。菲利普斯转而找到一位正在进行一系列实验的临床心理学家乔治·波考。几个星期之后,波考建议并鼓励菲利普斯律师与检察官一起解决这个问题,虽然当时他对这件事并不太担心。

1993年7月,波考收到佩恩母亲的来电,她说佩恩失踪了。波考联络了菲利普斯,菲利普斯首先想到的就是联系佩恩的前女友。随后他想到:他自己该怎么办?如果这样做,他就会破坏他与当事人之间的信任关系。一个小时后,菲利普斯的电话响了,是佩恩打来的。他说自己很长一段时间都在他前女友的房子周围乱转,并在墓地里与女孩已经过世的母亲聊天,听她从坟墓里传出的声音。心理医师波考意识到,佩恩现在的确是个危险人物,并有可能杀人或自杀。特别是佩恩的母亲告诉波考,佩恩曾提到过要杀死前女友和自己,波考认为道德义务应优先于法律责任。他把这个消息转告了菲利普斯,并说道:"勒罗伊,我知道你作为一个律师的责任,但我相信法律允许我做更多事。法律规定,如果我觉得当事人对他自己或对他人构成威胁时,我可以举报他。"

菲利普斯跟他的当事人说:"波考先生认为你病得很厉害,你需要帮助,并应该自首。他们会让你坐牢,但最终你会接受体检,以确认你是否应当进医院治疗。"佩恩对此表示同意后,菲利普斯告诫他,只需要跟医生说话,而不需要跟警察说什么。

Payne went to jail but refused to talk with police and because they had no hard evidence against him, Lanzo suggested to Phillips that they were ready to let him go. Phillips, by this time truly concerned about the safety of both Payne and his ex-girlfriend, responded, "If you turn him loose, the full responsibility is on you." When Payne called his attorney to say that he was back home, Phillips decided that the solution lay in bringing the situation to the media's attention and gaining the public's wrath. He also sent an investigator to visit Payne's girlfriend.

Media attention pushed the DA into action. When Phillips would not let his client confess outright, Lanzo suggested that Payne waive his confidentiality. This action would permit Bercaw to explain his findings without fear of moral and legal recriminations. Imagine everyone's astonishment when state psychologists found Phillips sane and competent to stand trial.

Phillips realized that he had bent too far. For safety's sake, he had yielded to the prosecutor's refusal to get Payne off the streets. He had probably violated the code of ethics for letting a client waive his rights and now faced reprimand from the Tennessee Bar Association's Board of Professional Responsibility. Bercaw, too, came in for his share of criticism for letting his client waive his constitutional rights; he received a warning letter from the Tennessee Psychological Association.

What knowledge about their clients should lawyers keep confidential?   ☞

佩恩进了监狱，但却拒绝与警方交谈，同时因为警方没有任何确凿的证据起诉他，兰佐告诉菲利普斯说他们准备让他出狱。现在菲利普斯真正关心的是佩恩前女友的安全，他跟兰佐说："如果你释放了他，那么你要负全责。"在佩恩打电话告诉律师他已经回到自己家里后，菲利普斯认为，真正解决这个问题的办法是让媒体关注整个事态的发展，并引发公众的愤怒。他还派了一位调查员去探访佩恩的前女友。

媒体的关注促使地方检察官采取了行动。菲利普斯不允许他的当事人直接公开供词，但兰佐却建议佩恩放弃他的隐私，这会使波考不再害怕面对冲突的道德和法律义务，并说出他的发现。想象一下，当州政府的心理学家发现佩恩（原文：菲利普斯）心理健全足以接受审判时每个人震惊的样子。

菲利普斯意识到自己有些矫枉过正了。为了安全起见，对检察官拒绝让佩恩入狱的决定，菲利普斯妥协了。他可能已经违反了让他的当事人放弃自己权利的道德准则，并面临来自田纳西州律师协会的职业责任委员会的谴责。波考也同样遭到了批评：他让他的当事人放弃了自身的宪法权利，并收到了田纳西州心理学会发出的警告信。

律师应当对他们当事人的哪些讯息保密？

IDENTIFYING BENEFITS AND COSTS

Group 1: Confidentiality Obligations of a Lawyer

1. List four or five possible consequences of requiring lawyers not to reveal their clients' confessions, except when the client' directly threatens to kill someone.

2. Write a B next to each consequence you consider to be a benefit and a C next to each cost.

3. Do you think the defense lawyer, Leroy Phillips, acted properly in this case? Why or why not? What do you think defense lawyers should be required to do in situations like this? Use the benefits and costs you have identified in developing your opinions.

Group 2: Confidentiality Obligations of a Therapist

1. List four or five possible consequences of requiring therapists not to reveal their clients' confessions, except when the client directly threatens to harm someone.

2. Write a B next to each consequence you consider to be a benefit and a C next to each cost.

3. Do you think the therapist, George Bercaw, acted properly in this case? Why or why not? What do you think therapists should be required to do in situations like this? Use the benefits and costs you have identified in developing your opinions.

Critical Thinking Exercise

EVALUATING, TAKING, AND DEFENDING A POSITION ON THE VIOLATION OF CONFIDENTIALITY

Imagine that the Tennessee Bar Association has charged Leroy Phillips with violating the ethical rules which prohibit lawyers from revealing their clients' secrets, and that the Tennessee Psychological Association has made similar charges against George Bercaw.

Administrative hearings are to be conducted by both organizations to deal with these charges. Group 1 will role-play the Bar Association hearing, and Group 2 will role-play the Psychological Association hearing. Each group should be divided into three parts, with one part assigned to play the role of hearing officers, one part assigned to play the role of advocates for the professional organization bringing the charges, and one part assigned to play the role of defense counsel for the accused individual.

识别隐私的利弊得失

第一组：律师的保密义务

1. 针对"除非当事人直接威胁要杀死某人，否则律师不得透露其供词"的规定，列出这项规定产生的结果。

2. 在你认为是利益的每种结果旁边标记"B"，在损失的旁边标上"C"。

3. 在这个案例中，你认为辩护律师勒罗伊·菲利普斯是否采取了适当的行动？为什么？为什么不？你认为在这样的情况下应该要求辩护律师做什么？运用你在第一题中找出的利弊得失，形成自己的观点。

第二组：临床心理医师的保密义务

1. 针对"除非当事人对他人构成直接威胁，否则医师不得透露其当事人供词"的规定，列出这项规定产生的结果。

2. 在你认为是利益的每种结果旁边标记"B"，在损失的旁边标上"C"。

3. 在这个案例中，你认为临床医师乔治·波考是否采取了适当的行动？为什么？为什么不？你认为在这样的情况下应该要求辩护律师做什么？运用你在第一题中找出的利弊得失，形成自己的观点。

重点思考练习

评估、选择和论证有关对隐私的侵犯问题

试假设，田纳西州律师协会起诉勒罗伊·菲利普斯违反了"禁止透露当事人秘密"的道德准则，同时田纳西州心理学会也对乔治·波考提出了类似指控。

两个协会准备召开行政听证会来处理这两项指控。第一组将召开模拟律师协会听证会，第二组将模拟心理学会的听证会。每一组都应再分为三个小组，一组同学扮演听证员，一组扮演赞成职业协会提起诉讼的支持者，最后一组扮演被告的辩护律师。

Advocates for the professional organizations should prepare arguments explaining why the accused individuals should be reprimanded or punished, and defense counsel for the accused individual should prepare arguments explaining why no discipline or punishment should be imposed. Each side should select one or two spokespersons to present its case.

While the advocates and defense counsel are preparing their arguments, the hearing officers should develop questions to ask each side, and should select a chairperson to conduct the hearing. Advocates for the professional organizations should make their presentations first; defense counsel should make their presentations second. Hearing officers may interrupt at any time to ask questions.

Each side should be allowed ten minutes for the presentation, including time spent asking and answering questions. After both sides have completed their presentations, the hearing officers should discuss the arguments presented, reach a decision, and explain their decision to the class.

Using the Lesson

1. Write a story or draw a picture that describes a time when having privacy was very important to you or to someone you know. Then list the benefits and costs of privacy in the story or picture you created. Finally, decide whether the benefits outweighed the costs, and explain why.

2. Draft a bill amending the Tennessee statute that makes it a crime for lawyers to reveal their clients' secrets, except when the client directly threatens to kill someone. Prepare arguments to support the changes your bill would make in the law.

　　职业协会的支持者们应该准备论据，解释为什么被告应受到谴责或惩罚；被告的辩护律师应准备论据，解释为什么被告不应该受到处分或惩罚。每一方都应该选择一个或两个发言人来陈述各方观点。

　　在协会的支持方以及被告的辩护律师正在准备自己的论据时，听证员应当列出要询问各方的问题，并应选出一位发言人主持听证会。职业协会的支持者应当首先发言，随后是被告的辩护律师。听证员可以在任何时候中断发言并提问。

　　每一方各有十分钟进行陈述，其中包括听证员提问和组员回答的时间。各方完成自己的陈述后，听证员应当讨论陈述中所提出的论据，做出决定，并向全班解释他们的决议。

知识运用

1. 写一个故事或画一幅画来描述对你或某个你认识的人来说，保护隐私非常重要的某个时刻，列出你的故事或画作中所涉及的隐私的利弊得失。然后权衡比较这些利弊得失，判断哪个更重要，并解释原因。

2. 草拟一项法案，修改田纳西州的法令，规定：除非当事人直接威胁要杀死某人，否则律师泄露当事人的秘密则被视为犯罪。准备论据来支持你的修改现有法规的提案。

LESSON 8

What Might Be Some Benefits and Costs of the Government Keeping a Secret?

Purpose of Lesson

This lesson provides an opportunity to examine the benefits and costs of allowing the federal government to keep secrets. Specifically, the lesson concerns a report on the Vietnam War which was "leaked" without authorization to reporters for the New York Times and the Washington Post. The lesson asks you to role-play a Supreme Court hearing in which the government seeks to prevent the newspapers from publishing the report.

When you have finished this lesson, you should be able to explain your position on the issue of privacy in this case. You also should be able to explain the usefulness of considering benefits and costs in evaluating, taking, and defending positions on issues of privacy.

Terms to Know

executive branch

injunction

prior restraint

Critical Thinking Exercise

EXAMINING GOVERNMENTAL PRIVACY

The following selection is based on an actual Supreme Court case, New York Times Co. v. United States, known as the Pentagon Papers case. Read the case carefully. After you have finished, the class will be divided into groups to evaluate the consequences of secrecy in the selection, and to engage in a simulated Supreme Court hearing on the case.

第八课：政府的保密行为可能带来哪些利弊得失？

本课目标

　　本课让我们有机会研究允许联邦政府保密的利弊得失。本课的具体内容是关于越南战争中一份未经授权"泄露"给《纽约时报》和《华盛顿邮报》记者的报告。本课要求你们模拟一场最高法院的听证会，在这场听证会上政府试图阻止报纸刊登这份报告。

　　学完本课后，你们应当能够解释在这个案例中自己对隐私问题的看法。你们也应该能说明在评估、选择和论证有关隐私问题的观点时，考虑隐私的利弊得失有什么用途。

掌握词汇

行政部门

禁制令

预先制止令（译者注：司法上预先禁止公布某项陈述或表达意见）

重点思考练习

研究政府的隐私

以下阅读材料来自最高法院的真实个案："纽约时报公司诉美利坚合众国"，该案又以"五角大楼文件案"著称。仔细阅读该案例，全班将被分成若干小组来评估案例中隐私所产生的结果，然后模拟最高法院召开针对此案的听证会。

The Pentagon Papers Case

American involvement in the Vietnam War generated massive conflict in the United States. By 1967 more than 35,000 Americans had been killed or wounded or were missing in action, and many Americans publicly expressed their opposition to the war. President Johnson's commitment to increase the number of troops overseas to more than 500,000 by the middle of 1968 led to increased nationwide protests. At the 1968 Democratic National Convention thousands of anti-war protesters clashed with the Chicago police; the protests grew even larger after President Nixon took office. In December, 1969, 250,000 anti-war protesters demonstrated in Washington, D.C., to oppose Nixon's plans for only a gradual withdrawal of U.S. troops, and thousands more participated in anti-war rallies around the country. Some demonstrations led to violent conflict. National Guard troops called in to maintain order at Kent State University in Ohio shot and killed four students on May 4, 1970, and on May 14, 1970, state police shot and killed two students at Jackson State College in Mississippi.

In June, 1971, The New York Times and the Washington Post obtained copies of a classified 7,000-page report entitled "History of U.S. Decision-Making Process on Vietnam Policy." The report, which showed that the government had misled the American public about U.S. involvement in Vietnam, was leaked by Daniel Ellsberg, a former government employee, without authorization. When the newspapers began to publish excerpts from the report, the government sued for an injunction-a court order prohibiting certain conduct-to prevent further publication of the report.

 Daniel Ellsberg arguably broke the law by providing the "Pentagon Papers" report to The New York Times and the Washington Post. Does that make a difference in whether the government should be able to prevent publication of the report?   ☞

五角大楼文件案

卷入越南战争后美国国内爆发了大规模冲突。到 1967 年，已有超过 3 万 5 千名美国人死亡、受伤或在战事行动中失踪，许多美国人公开表示反对这场战争。从约翰逊总统承诺增加海外派兵人数直至 1968 年中期，有超过 50 万美国士兵被派驻海外，也激发了越来越多的全国性抗议活动。在 1968 年的民主党全国代表大会上，成千上万的反战示威者与芝加哥警察发生了剧烈冲突。而在尼克松总统上台后，抗议者的阵容扩大了。1969 年 12 月，25 万名反战示威者在华盛顿特区游行，抗议尼克松仅仅要求美军"逐步"从越南撤退的计划，数以千计的人们更踊跃地参与到全国各地的反战集会中。一些示威游行活动引发了暴力冲突，国民警卫队应召前来维持俄亥俄州肯特州立大学的秩序，1970 年 5 月 4 日 4 名学生被枪杀。1970 年 5 月 14 日，密西西比州警察开枪打死了两名杰克逊州立大学的学生。

1971 年 6 月，《纽约时报》和《华盛顿邮报》得到一份长达 7000 页、题为《美国的越南战争决策史》的机密报告的副本。该报告揭露了政府在美国参加越南战争问题上对公众的误导，文件是一位曾经是政府雇员的丹尼尔·埃尔斯伯格擅自泄露的。当报纸开始连载该报告后，政府向法院起诉，请求一项禁制令（法院下令禁止某些行为）以阻止报纸继续刊登该报告。

按理说，丹尼尔·埃尔斯伯格将"五角大楼文件"披露给《纽约时报》和《华盛顿邮报》是违法的。这对决定政府是否应当有能力阻止公布该报告的问题有影响吗？

The government claimed that publication of the classified report would endanger lives, undermine efforts to negotiate a peace treaty, and interfere with efforts to secure the release of prisoners of war. The government argued that the responsibility of the executive branch for the security of the nation is so basic that the president should be granted an injunction against publication of a newspaper story whenever the information to be revealed threatens grave and irreparable injury to the public interest, regardless of how the newspaper got the information it seeks to publish.

The newspapers claimed that the First Amendment prohibits any prior restraint on the publication of news, whatever the source; that the main purpose of the First Amendment was to prohibit the widespread practice of governmental suppression of embarrassing information and to safeguard the freedom of the press to criticize and expose deception in the government. The newspapers argued that the information they sought to publish would contribute to an ongoing national debate concerning the Vietnam War; that open debate and discussion of public issues are essential to preserve our constitutional form of self-government; that secrecy in government is undemocratic and perpetuates bureaucratic errors; and that the government's concerns about the possible effects of publishing the report were unproven speculations.

Conducting a Supreme Court Hearing

Your class should be organized into three groups to conduct the following activity. One group will play the role of Supreme Court justices, one group will play the role of lawyers for the newspapers, and one group will play the role of lawyers for the government. Each of the groups should list the benefits and costs of allowing the government to maintain secrecy in the above situation by prohibiting the newspapers from publishing the secret report. The groups representing lawyers for the newspapers and for the government should prepare a brief presentation explaining why the government should or should not be permitted to keep the report secret. Use the benefits and costs you have listed in preparing your arguments. Select two or three spokespersons to present the group's position to the Supreme Court.

While the other groups are preparing their presentations, the students representing Supreme Court justices should prepare questions to ask the spokespersons for each side, and should select a Chief Justice to conduct the hearing.

政府声称，刊登这份机密报告会危及生命、破坏和平条约谈判的努力、并干扰政府在确保释放战俘方面的努力。政府认为，行政部门的根本职责就是保障国家安全。无论何时泄露这些信息都会为公众利益带来严重威胁和无法弥补的伤害，应当授予总统颁布禁制令，阻止公开这则新闻报告，无论这些报社是如何获得这些即将发表的信息的。

报社则认为，宪法第一修正案禁止任何对新闻出版的限制，不论新闻来源是什么；第一修正案的主要目的就是要禁止政府通常压制难堪信息的做法，以保障新闻媒体批评和揭露政府欺骗行为的自由。报社认为，他们试图发表的信息，将有助于推动现在正在进行的关于越南战争问题的全国大辩论，公共问题的公开辩论和讨论对维护美国自治政府的宪法形式来说是至关重要的。报社认为政府保密是不民主的，延续了官僚主义的错误，并认为政府所提出的公布该报告可能产生影响的观点，只是未经证实的猜测。

模拟进行最高法院听证会

你们班将分成三组进行以下活动，第一组将扮演最高法院的法官，第二组将扮演报社的辩护律师，最后一组扮演政府的辩护律师。各组都并应列出上述案例中允许政府通过禁止报社刊登秘密报告来保密所产生的利弊得失。代表报社律师的小组和代表政府律师的小组应当准备一份简短的陈述，解释为什么应该或为什么不应该允许政府保护秘密报告。运用各组自己列出的利弊得失来论证各方观点。选出两个或三个发言人向最高法院陈述各自小组的观点。

其他各组在准备自己的发言陈述时，扮演最高法院法官的学生小组应该准备问各方发言人的问题，并应选出一位主审法官来主持听证会。

After each group has presented its position, the Supreme Court justices should discuss the arguments presented and decide whether to allow the government to keep the report secret. The justices should justify their decision in terms of the benefits and costs it will entail. The class should conclude the activity by discussing the usefulness of considering benefits and costs in taking and defending positions on issues regarding privacy and other subjects.

Using the Lesson

1. Should the government be allowed to prevent the publication of information on how to make a nuclear bomb? Research the court case of United States v. Progressive, Inc. and report to the class how one court dealt with this issue. Explain why you agree or disagree with the court's decision.

2. Can you think of any institution (such as a school, hospital, or government agency) that has information about you or your friends that you would not want to be made public? If so, do you approve of this example of institutional secrecy? Explain your position.

3. Review the questions you wrote in your privacy notebook or journal at the end of Lesson 5. What do you think the answers to these questions might be? Write your answers down, then list three or more new questions you have about privacy.

在各组陈述完各自观点后,最高法院的法官应该讨论各组陈述的论据,并判断是否允许政府对秘密报告保密。法官应当根据可能产生的利弊得失来论证自己的决定。全班应当总结此次活动,讨论在选择、论证隐私和其他相关问题的观点时,权衡考虑利弊得失的实用性。

知识运用

1.　是否应当允许政府组织发布有关如何制造核弹的信息?阅读并研究"美利坚合众国诉进步杂志案"的法院判例,向全班报告当时法庭如何判定此案。解释为什么你同意或不同意法院的判决。

2.　想想有什么公共机构(如学校、医院或政府机构)掌握了一些你或你的朋友不想公开的信息?如果有,你会赞成这种机构保密吗?解释你的观点。

3.　回顾第五课结束时你写在笔记本或日记上的问题,你认为这些问题的答案会是什么?把它们写下来,然后列出三个或更多关于隐私的新问题。

Unit Four
What Should Be the Scope and Limits of Privacy?

Purpose of Unit

Some of the most important issues we face as citizens involve questions about the scope and limits of privacy What kinds of things will we allow people to keep private? When will we require privacy to give way to other values? Issues such as these arise between individuals or groups wishing to maintain privacy and others claiming the right to know something private or to regulate or interfere with an individual's or a group's freedom. In some cases it is reasonable and fair to protect privacy; at other times different values and interests may be more important. In this unit you will learn some intellectual tools-concepts and procedures-that are useful in evaluating, taking, and defending positions on questions about the scope and limits of privacy.

第四单元：隐私的范围和限制应当是什么？

单元目标

　　隐私的范围和限制问题，是作为公民的我们所面临的最重要的问题之一。我们会允许人们对哪些事情保密呢？什么时候我们需要牺牲隐私，向其他价值让步？当有个人或群体希望保密时，另一边就会有人宣布自己有权知道某些隐私、有权管制或干预个人或团体的自由，上述有关隐私的问题就会出现。在某些情况下，保护隐私是合理且公平的，但在另外一些情况下，其他不同的价值和利益可能比隐私更重要。在本单元中你们将会学到一些知识工具（包括概念和程序），有助于评估、选择和论证针对隐私的范围和限制问题的某些观点。

 How do these photographs illustrate different issues concerning the scope and limits of privacy?

这些照片如何体现了关于隐私的范围和限制的不同问题？

LESSON 9

What Considerations Are Useful in Dealing with Issues of Privacy?

Purpose of Lesson

This lesson introduces you to some considerations useful in dealing with issues of privacy, and provides an opportunity for you to apply these considerations in examining a conflict between privacy and the need to enforce the law. When you have finished the lesson, you should be able to explain how these considerations can be useful in examining issues of privacy.

Terms to Know

effects	consent
Freedom of information Act	moral obligation
legality	interests
legal obligation	seizure
warrant	relevant considerations
values	

When should government be able to invade your privacy?

Since colonial times, Americans have believed strongly that citizens should have a right to privacy protecting them from arbitrary arrest and unreasonable searches, and protecting their homes from forced entry by government officials. The Fourth Amendment to the United States Constitution prohibits "unreasonable searches and seizures" by the government of our "persons, houses, papers, and effects [possessions]." However, it is not always easy to agree on what is unreasonable.

第九课：考虑哪些因素有助于处理隐私问题？

本课目标

　　本课将介绍某些有助于处理隐私问题的考虑因素，使你们有机会在处理隐私和执行法律的需要之间的冲突时，运用这些考虑因素。学完本课后，你们应该能够说明在研究隐私问题时考虑这些因素是如何发挥作用的。

掌握词汇

财产	同意
信息自由法	道德义务
合法性	利益
法律责任	扣押
授权	相关考虑因素
价值观	

政府在什么时候可以侵犯你的隐私？

　　从殖民时期开始，美国人一直坚持相信公民应当有隐私权，保护自己不被任意逮捕和无理搜查，保护自己的住房不被政府官员强行进入。美国宪法第四修正案禁止政府对美国公民的"人身、住宅、文件和财产"进行"无理的搜查和扣押"。然而，关于什么是"无理"的问题，人们却并不那么容易达成共识。

The Constitution's protection of privacy is not absolute. Government officials are allowed to enter our homes under certain conditions. For example, firefighters may enter our homes to put out a fire. Police may enter our homes if necessary to stop a crime in progress or one about to be committed. Police also may enter our homes if they first convince a judge that there is good reason to believe evidence of a crime will be found inside, and the judge issues a search warrant authorizing them to search for that evidence. Government officials also may enter someone's home if that person gives them permission or invites them inside.

Outside the home, people's expectations of privacy are not as strong. Still, the Fourth Amendment prohibits police and other government officials from unreasonably infringing on people's right to privacy. Although an officer who sees something suspicious does not need to obtain a warrant to stop and question the persons involved, he or she cannot stop and question a person arbitrarily, or just on a hunch. The conduct of the officer must be reasonable in order to comply with the Fourth Amendment

 Should we always require a warrant for government officials to enter our homes? What examples might you cite to support your position?   ☞

　　宪法对隐私权的保护并不是绝对的，政府官员允许在某种特定条件下进入我们的住宅。例如，为扑灭火灾消防队员可以进入人们家里；如果为了阻止正在进行的犯罪或即将发生的罪行，警察也可以进入人们的住宅。此外，如果警方有充分理由说服法官相信，在某个房子里可以找到犯罪证据，并请法官发出搜查令授权警方寻找犯罪证据，那么警察也可以进入居民住宅。如果事先得到房屋主人的允许或邀请，政府官员也可以进入民宅。

　　在住宅之外，人们对隐私的期望就不那么强烈了。但联邦宪法第四修正案仍然禁止警察和其他政府官员无理侵犯民众的隐私权。一位政府官员如果发现了某些可疑现象，不需要取得搜查令就可以制止并询问当事人；但他或她不能任意地，或仅凭预感就拦住某个人进行盘问。政府官员的行为必须合理，并符合联邦宪法第四修正案。

我们是否总应要求政府官员在有授权的情况下进入我们的住宅？你会举什么例子来论证自己的观点？

Critical Thinking Exercise

IDENTIFYING THE CONFLICTING VALUES AND INTERESTS OF THE FOURTH AMENDMENT

As you read the following situation, think about the values and interests promoted by the Fourth Amendment, the competing values and interests at stake, and the choice that must be made between them. Work with a study partner to answer the "What do you think?" questions.

Jack Frost: Citizen and Suspected Criminal

Jack Frost is a citizen of the United States. Privacy is an important part of his life: it means that he is secure in his home; he can cast a secret ballot at election time; and he can think about any idea without fear that the government will try to make him conform to its point of view. Without privacy, his and all other Americans' individuality and freedom would mean very little.

Jack Frost is a suspected leader of organized crime. He may be responsible for millions of dollars in theft, drug dealing on a massive scale, scores of injuries and murders, and countless other violations of the law. The police want to end the suspected criminal career of Jack Frost, but to do so, they need information about his activities. Their job is very difficult because of every person's right of privacy.

What do you think?

1. What values and interests conflict with privacy in the situation described above?

2. Why might it be necessary to choose between protecting privacy and protecting other values?

3. Why is it important to have rules or a system for deciding when someone's right to privacy should give way to other values?

重点思考练习

找出第四修正案中相互冲突的价值和利益

阅读下文，思考联邦宪法第四修正案所倡导的价值和利益，以及案例中急需调解的相互冲突的价值和利益，我们必须在这些价值和利益中做出选择。与一位同学合作回答"你怎么看？"这一部分的问题。

杰克・弗罗斯特：公民与嫌疑犯

杰克・弗罗斯特是一位美国公民。隐私是他生活中很重要的一部分：这意味着他在自己的家里是安全的；他可以在选举时选择不记名投票；他可以思考任何事情，而无需害怕政府会强迫他一定要与政府的观点一致。假使没有了隐私，他和所有其他美国人所拥有的个性和自由将变得没有任何意义。

同时，杰克・弗罗斯特是一起有组织犯罪的嫌犯和组织者，他的身上可能背负着无数罪行：偷窃数百万美元、大规模毒品交易、几十人受伤、谋杀以及其他犯罪行为。警方希望终结杰克・弗罗斯特涉嫌犯罪的职业生涯，但如此一来他们需要更多有关他的活动的信息。然而，因为每个人都有隐私权，警察的工作就变得非常艰巨。

你怎么看？

1. 上述阅读材料中涉及了哪些与隐私冲突的价值与利益？
2. 为什么我们必须在"保护隐私"和"保护其他价值"之间做出选择？
3. 在决定一个人的隐私是否应当对其他价值妥协的时候，为什么设立某些规则或制度来做决定是非常重要的？

What things should you consider in analyzing issues of privacy?

As you can see, privacy may interfere with other important values and interests. In the situation you just considered, a conflict existed between the goals of protecting privacy and enforcing the law. In any given situation, people may have different opinions about how conflicts between privacy and other values and interests should be resolved. Following are some relevant considerations-things that should be considered, that are important, or that might make a difference-in deciding how to resolve conflicts about privacy.

Consent. Has someone whose privacy is at issue consented or agreed to the invasion of his or her privacy? For example:

- If police want to search someone's home or car, and the person gives them permission to do so, the person has consented to the search.

- At airport security checks, airline passengers know that they will have to pass through a metal detector, and carry-on luggage will be x-rayed, before they can board the plane. Because they know this in advance, and because they could avoid the invasion of their privacy by choosing not to travel by plane, it can be said that they have consented to these security procedures.

- Elected officials know that much of their personal history and behavior will be revealed to the public. Because they could avoid this invasion of their privacy by choosing not to run for public office, it might be said that they have consented to the public disclosure of information about themselves.

Legality. Do those who wish to invade someone's privacy have a legal right-a right confirmed by law-to do so? For example:

- A search warrant issued by a judge gives police a legal right to search the places described in the search warrant.

- Customs officials have a legal right to search anyone who crosses the border into the United States.

- The Freedom of information Act, a law passed by Congress in 1966, gives people a legal right to obtain documents from the federal government, unless the documents contain certain types of confidential or classified information.

分析隐私问题时应该考虑什么？

正如你们所看到的，隐私可能会干扰其他重要的价值和利益。在上述情况中，"保护隐私的目标"和"执行法律的目标"之间就存在着冲突。在任何特定情况下，针对如何解决隐私和其他价值与利益之间的冲突，人们往往都有不同看法。以下是人们在决定如何解决关于隐私权的冲突时的某些相关考虑因素（应该考虑的因素、重要的或可能产生影响的因素）。

1. **同意**：隐私权处于争议中的当事人是否同意他或她的隐私受到侵犯？例如：

   · 如果警察要搜查某人的住宅或汽车，而当事人也允许他们这样做，这就意味着当事人已经同意了此次搜查。

   在机场进行安全检查时，乘坐飞机的乘客知道，在登机之前他们必须通过金属探测器的检查，同时随身携带的行李也要经过 X 光检查。

   · 因为乘客事先知道要进行安检，同时可以选择不搭飞机以避免自己的隐私权受到侵犯，因此可以说，乘客已经同意进行安全检查。

   · 选举产生的政府官员明白，他们过去很多个人经历和行为都会向公众披露。因为他们可以选择不参加公职的竞选，以避免自己的隐私受到侵犯，因此也可以说，他们已经同意向公众披露自己的相关信息。

2. **合法性**：要侵犯他人隐私的人是否拥有某种合法权利（一种由法律确认的权利）这样做？例如：

   · 一项由法官签发给警察的搜查令，赋予了警察对搜查令中描述的地方进行搜查的合法权利。

   海关官员拥有合法权利搜查任何入境者。

   · 1966 年美国国会通过的《信息自由法》，赋予了美国人民获得联邦政府文件的合法权利，除非这些文件中包含了某些类型的秘密或机密信息。

Legal obligation. Does a person have a legal obligation-a responsibility imposed or enforced by law-to maintain the privacy of another? For example:

- Certain laws impose a legal obligation on alcohol and drug abuse counselors not to disclose their clients' identities.

- If someone signs a contract promising to keep certain information secret, the contract may create a legal obligation not to reveal the information.

- Under the Constitution, police have a legal obligation not to invade a person's privacy without a warrant, except in certain limited circumstances.

Moral obligation. Does a person have a moral obligation-a responsibility imposed by principles of right and wrong-to maintain the privacy of another? For example:

- Someone who promises to keep a secret generally has a moral obligation not to tell the secret to anyone else.

- Doctors have a moral obligation not to reveal private medical information about their patients, and counselors have a moral obligation not to reveal what people tell them in private.

- Lawyers have a moral obligation not to reveal confidential information about their clients.

 What do you think are the costs and benefits of expecting public officials to disclose information about themselves?   ☞

3. **法律义务**：一个人是否有法律义务（由法律判定或强制施加的责任）去保护其他人的隐私？例如：

   • 某些法律要求治疗酒精和药物滥用问题的心理辅导师不得披露病人的身份。

   • 如果有人签署合同，承诺对某些信息保密，该合同就产生了一种不得透露该信息的法律义务。

   • 根据联邦宪法规定，警方有法律义务不得在没有授权的情况下侵犯某个人的隐私，除非在某些有限定的情况下。

4. **道德义务**：一个人是否有道德义务（一种由是非准则规定的责任）去保护其他人的隐私？例如：

   • 承诺保守秘密的人通常有道德义务不向任何其他人透露秘密的内容。

   • 医生有道德义务不泄露病人的个人病历信息，心理辅导师也有道德义务不向外界透露客户与他们私下的交谈内容。

   • 律师有道德义务不透露有关当事人的私密信息。

你认为期待公职人员透露个人信息会带来什么利弊得失？

Critical Thinking Exercise

DESCRIBING RELEVANT CONSIDERATIONS

As you read the following selection adapted from the case of Terry v. Ohio, think about the values and interests listed in the previous section. Work in small groups to answer the "What do you think?" questions.

The Search

Officer Martin McFadden thought something was odd about the behavior of two men talking across the street. First one and then the other walked up the street, looked into a store window, walked a short distance, turned around, stopped again in front of the same store, and then rejoined his companion. Back and forth, almost a dozen times, the men repeated this pattern of behavior. Then both men walked toward the store.

"Stop right there," Officer McFadden shouted. "Put your hands against the wall and spread your legs."

The men complied. Officer McFadden patted down the suspects. He was not surprised to feel a hard, heavy object concealed in each man's overcoat. These objects proved to be guns.

"You're under arrest," he informed them. Later charged with carrying a concealed weapon, John Terry and Richard Chilton were represented by a skilled lawyer. Told of the circumstances of his clients' arrest, the lawyer argued that Officer McFadden's conduct violated the Fourth Amendment. Therefore, the evidence against Mr. Terry and Mr. Chilton should not be used in court.

The prosecutor disagreed. "Officer McFadden had a reasonable suspicion that criminal activity was afoot," he argued. "Mr. Terry and Mr. Chilton were 'casing' the store and were about to commit armed robbery. Officer McFadden had every right to stop the men and to frisk them for weapons they might use to attack him."

重要思考练习

描述相关考虑因素

阅读以下选自"特里诉俄亥俄州案"的材料，思考上文中所列出的价值和利益。分成小组讨论，并回答"你怎么看？"这一部分的问题。

搜身

警官马丁·麦克法登认为，对街两个男人说话的样子很古怪。一个人在前，另一个也随后跟上。一个人先走到街上一家商店门口，透过窗户往里看。向前走了不远，又转过身来，再次停在同一家商店前，和他的同伴会合。来来回回几乎十几趟，他们不断重复这样做。

然后，当两人又朝商店走去的时候，麦克法登警官叫住了他们："停在那儿，"麦克法登喊道："把手放在墙上，腿打开站好。"

于是两个男人照他说的做。警官麦克法登拍了拍两个嫌犯的身体，感觉到两个人的大衣底下都藏着很硬且厚实的东西，对此他并不惊讶。后来的事实证明，他们藏着的这些东西是枪。

"你们被捕了，"警官告诉他们。约翰·特里和理查德·奇尔顿随后以携带和隐藏武器被起诉，并由一位经验丰富的辩护律师为他们辩护。在听到他的两位当事人被捕的情况后，律师认为，警官麦克法登的行为违反了宪法第四修正案，因此，那些对特里先生和奇尔顿先生不利的证据不得在法庭上使用。

检察官对此表示了反对："警官麦克法登有理由怀疑他们正在进行犯罪活动，"他说："特里先生和奇尔顿先生是在商店外面'踩点'，并准备实施持枪抢劫。警官麦克法登有全权制止他们，并对他们进行搜身，以寻找可能用来攻击他的武器。"

What do you think?

1. Did Mr. Terry and Mr. Chilton consent to the search by Officer McFadden? Explain your answer.

2. Did Officer McFadden have a legal right to search Mr. Terry and Mr. Chilton? Why or why not?

3. Did Officer McFadden have a legal obligation not to search Mr. Terry and Mr. Chilton? Why or why not?

4. Did Officer McFadden have a moral obligation not to search Mr. Terry and Mr. Chilton? Why or why not?

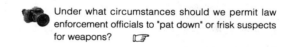 Under what circumstances should we permit law enforcement officials to "pat down" or frisk suspects for weapons?

你怎么看?

1. 特里先生和奇尔顿先生是否同意了警官麦克法登对他们搜身？解释你的答案。

2. 警官麦克法登是否有合法权利对特里先生和奇尔顿先生进行搜身？为什么？为什么不？

3. 警官麦克法登有法律义务不对特里先生和奇尔顿先生进行搜身吗？为什么？为什么不？

4. 警官麦克法登有道德义务不对特里先生和奇尔顿先生进行搜身吗？为什么？为什么不？

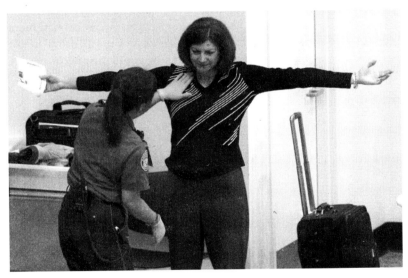

在什么情况下我们应该允许执法人员"拍身检查"嫌犯并对其搜身查找武器？

Using the Lesson

1.If you believe that police never should be allowed to invade people's privacy, then how can society be protected against crime? If you believe that police always should be allowed to invade people's privacy, then how can a person feel secure and be free? If you think that police should be allowed to invade people's privacy only in certain situations, then what rules would you impose on police to tell them when the are allowed to invade someone's privacy?

2. Think about a conflict involving privacy in your school, neighborhood, or town. Use what you have learned in this lesson to evaluate this conflict. Imagine alternative ways in which the conflict might be resolved. Decide what is the best way to resolve the conflict. Then explain to the class what the conflicts, what should be done about the conflict, and why.

3.Working with your teacher, invite a person who deals with issues of privacy, such as a police officer, judge, doctor, lawyer, or city council member, to visit your classroom. Ask that person to describe a conflict involving privacy and to suggest several ways in which the conflict could be resolved.

知识运用

1. 如果你认为根本就不应该允许警察侵犯人们的隐私，那么社会该如何打击犯罪、保障社会安全呢？如果你认为应当允许警察随时可以侵犯人们的隐私，那么一个人要怎样才能感到安全和自由？如果你认为应当允许警察只在某些特定情况下侵犯人们的隐私，那么你会给警察制定什么样的规则，让他们明确何时才被允许侵犯某人的隐私？

2. 想想在你的学校、居住的小区或城市里发生的有关隐私的冲突。运用本课学到的知识，来评估这一冲突。想想有没有什么可以解决这一冲突的备选方案，判断解决这一冲突最好的方法是哪种。然后向全班同学说明你思考的这个有关隐私的冲突是什么，应当做哪些事来解决冲突以及为什么要这么做。

3. 与老师一起邀请一个处理隐私相关问题的人，例如警察、法官、医生、律师或市议会议员，来你们班座谈。请他或她描述一种涉及隐私的冲突，并提出可以解决这一冲突的几种方式。

LESSON 10

What Conflicts about Privacy May Arise from Law Enforcement?

Purpose of Lesson

In this lesson you learn and apply set of intellectual tools to examine an issue regarding law enforcement. The issue is whether the police should have the authority to demand that a person state his or her name, and to arrest the person if he or she refuses. When you have completed the lesson, you should be able to use the intellectual tools to take and defend a position on this issue of privacy.

Term to Know

loitering

What are procedures for analyzing issues of privacy?

In the last lesson you looked at some relevant considerations that can help you think more clearly about issues of privacy; now you will use these considerations as part of a specific procedure for analyzing issues of privacy. The procedure is described below and summarized in the chart on page 142,144; it consists of series of steps that you can follow each time you want to evaluate, take, or defend a position on privacy. Note that the person in each step might be a group or an institution, such as a school or government agency.

1. Identify the person claiming privacy. Identify the person who wants privacy and what he or she wants to keep private. How is it to be kept private? What are the reasons for wanting to keep it private?

2. Identify the person wishing to invade the other's privacy. Identify the person who opposes the first person's claim to privacy. Give the reasons for opposing the claim. Describe the way in which the first person's privacy is to be invaded.

第十课：执行法律时会出现哪些有关隐私的冲突？

本课目标

在本课中，你们将学习和运用一套知识工具，来研究与法律执行相关的问题。这一问题是：警方是否应当有权要求一个人说出自己的名字，如果他或她拒绝，警察是否有权逮捕他（她）。学完本课后，你们应该能够运用知识工具针对类似隐私问题选择和论证自己的观点。

掌握词汇

逗留

分析隐私问题的程序是什么？

在上一课中，你们已经学习了一些有助于更清晰地思考隐私问题的相关考虑因素；现在你们将运用这些考虑因素，作为一种特定程序的一部分来分析隐私问题。下文中对这一程序进行了描述，并用第 143、145 页的图表对这一程序进行了概括；这个程序中包含了一系列步骤，针对有关隐私的观点，你们可以按照这些步骤来进行评估、选择或论证。请注意，每个步骤中的对象可以是一个人，也可能是一个团体或公共机构，例如学校或政府机构。

1. 找出要求隐私的对象。找出某个需要隐私的对象，以及他或她希望保密的事情是什么。这件事要如何保密？他们希望对这件事保密的原因是什么？

2. 找出希望侵犯他人隐私的对象。找出某个反对以上隐私要求的对象，说明他们反对这一隐私要求的原因，描述以上第一人的隐私会受到怎

3. Examine relevant considerations. Consider matters that are relevant to or make a difference in conflicts about privacy, such as consent, legality, legal obligations, and moral obligations. Determine how these matters apply to the situation.

4. Evaluate alternative means of managing the issue. Think about different ways to resolve the issue. These might include recognizing or rejecting the claim to privacy or reaching a compromise. In thinking about these alternatives, be sure to identify and evaluate the costs and benefits of each proposed solution.

5. Take and defend a position. Decide what you think is the best way to resolve the issue and explain the reasons for your decision.

Critical Thinking Exercise

EVALUATING A POSITION ON LAW ENFORCEMENT

As you read the following situation, think about how you would feel if a police officer asked you to stop and identify yourself. Then work in small groups to answer the questions on the intellectual tool chart that follows. Be prepared to explain your answers to the class.

样的侵犯。

　　3. 研究相关考虑因素。在有关隐私的冲突中，考虑相关的或对冲突产生影响的因素，例如同意、合法性、法律义务和道德义务。决定应当如何将这些考虑因素运用到冲突的具体情况中。

　　4. 评估处理问题的备选方案。想想可以解决这一问题的不同方式，其中可能包括：承认第一人对隐私的要求、拒绝这一要求、在两者之间的折衷方案。在思考这些可选方法时，一定要找出每个预选方案的利弊得失并进行评估。

　　5. 选择和论证自己的观点。选择一种你认为解决这一冲突最好的方法，并对自己的选择做出解释。

重点思考练习

评估有关法律执行的观点

　　阅读下文时，想想如果在大街上，遇到一个警察要求你站住，并让你当众说出自己的名字，你会有什么感觉。分成小组讨论，并回答"知识产权工具图表"中的问题。准备向全班解释你的答案。

The Stranger

Throughout the history of civilization, communities have sought to protect themselves from outsiders. Yet one of the cherished freedoms we enjoy as Americans is the right to go where we please and to travel from town to town. Not too long ago, these two traditions came into conflict in California.

Police officers stopped Edward Lawson as he walked down the street. Asked to identify himself, Mr. Lawson refused to cooperate, remaining silent. California law made it a crime for a person who loiters or wanders upon the streets or from place to place without apparent reason or business to refuse to identify himself and to account for his presence when requested by a police officer. The police arrested Mr. Lawson and charged him with violating this law. Mr. Lawson sued to have the law declared unconstitutional. He claimed that the law violated his constitutional privacy rights guaranteed by the Fourth Amendment. His case eventually reached the United States Supreme Court.

 Would you rather live in a society where police could stop anyone on the street and demand identification, or in a society where they could not?

陌生人

在整个人类文明史中，共同体一直在寻求保护自己不受外来入侵的方式。然而，作为美国人的我们所享有的宝贵的自由之一，就是去任何我们想去的地方的权利，以及在城镇之间穿梭旅行的权利。就在不久之前，这两种传统却在加利福尼亚州陷入了冲突之中。

爱德华·劳森走在街上的时候，被一名警官拦住。在被问到有关身份问题时，劳森先生拒绝合作并保持沉默。加州法律规定，如果一个人没有明确的理由或事情，在街上逗留或徘徊，且拒绝向警察说明自己的身份，或解释自己出现在此地的原因，都将被视为犯罪。警方逮捕了劳森先生，并控告他违反了此项法规。劳森先生向法院起诉这项法规违宪。他认为，这项法规违反了联邦宪法第四修正案保障的他的隐私权。此案件最终提交至美国最高法院审理。

你会选择生活在一个警察可以在街上拦住任何人并要求确认其身份的社会，还是一个警察无法这样做的地方？

Using the Lesson

1. Suppose Congress was considering a law that would require every person to carry a "National ID" card specifying whether the person is a U.S. citizen or the citizen of another country. The law would require that people present the card when seeking employment. What do you think would be the best arguments for and against such a law? What position would you take on such a law? Write a letter to your member of Congress expressing your views. Be sure to explain the reasons for your position.

2. Government agencies have used television cameras to monitor public places such as highway rest areas, parking garages, and subway stations. How do you think this compares to having police officers patrolling such areas? Which provides better protection against unlawful behavior? Which imposes a greater burden on privacy? Do you agree with the government's use of cameras in this way? Write a letter to the editor of a newspaper or give a presentation to your class expressing your opinions.

知识运用

1. 假设国会正在审议一项法律，该法律要求每个人都必须随身携带"公民身份证"，证明这个人是美国公民还是其他国家的公民。同时该法律规定人们在找工作的时候也必须出示身份证。你认为支持或反对该项法律最好使用什么论据？针对这项法律，你的观点是什么？写一封信给一位国会议员，说明你自己的观点，请记住，一定要说明你的看法的理由。

2. 政府机构早已采用电视摄像机监视某些公共区域，例如高速公路休息区、停车场、地铁站。相比警察在这些区域进行巡逻，你怎么看待这种电视监控系统？以上哪一种方式可以为杜绝非法行为提供更好的安全保障？哪一种给隐私带来了更大的负担？你是否同意政府用这种方式使用摄像机？写一封信给一个报社的编辑或向全班做一次报告，说明你对上述问题的看法。

Intellectual Tool Chart for Issues of Privacy	
Questions	**Answers**
1. Identify the person claiming privacy: • Whose claim to privacy was endangered in this case? • What objects did the person want to keep private? • How might the person have kept the object private? • Why might the person want to keep the objects private?	
2. Identify the person wishing to limit or invade the other's privacy: • Who wished to limit or invade the other's privacy? • How did that person invade the other's privacy? • Why did that person want to invade the other's privacy?	
3. Examine relevant considerations: • Did the person consent to have his or her privacy invaded? Explain. • Did the person who invaded the other's privacy have a legal right to do so? Why or why not? • Did the person who invaded the other's privacy have a legal obligation not to do so? Why or why not? • Did the person who invaded the other's privacy have a moral obligation not to do so? Why or why not?	

隐私知识工具图	
问题	答案
1. 找出要求隐私的对象： · 在这个案例中谁声称自己的隐私权受到了威胁？ · 他们想要保密的内容是什么？ · 他们可以怎样将这件事保密？ · 他们希望保密的原因会是什么？	
2. 找出希望侵犯他人隐私的对象： · 谁希望限制或侵犯他人的隐私？ · 他们怎样侵犯了他人的隐私？ · 为什么他们要侵犯他人的隐私？	
3. 研究相关考虑因素： · 第一人是否同意自己的隐私被侵犯？请解释。 · 侵犯他人隐私的人是否有合法权利这么做？ 　为什么有？为什么没有？ · 侵犯他人隐私的人是否有法律义务不这么做？为什么有？为什么没有？ · 侵犯他人隐私的人是否有道德义务不这么做？为什么有？为什么没有？	

Questions	Answers
4. Evaluate alternative means of managing the issue: • What are the costs and benefits of recognizing the person's claim to privacy? • What are the costs and benefits of rejecting the claim to privacy? • What are alternative means of gathering information that the person who wants to invade the privacy of another might use? • What are the benefits of each of these means? • What are the costs of each of these means?	
5. Take and defend a position: • How do you think this issue should be resolved? Explain your position.	

问题	答案
4. 评估处理问题的备选方案： ·认可第一人对隐私的要求会带来什么利弊得失？ ·拒绝他们对隐私的要求会带来什么利弊得失？ ·想要侵犯他人隐私的人可以运用哪些方法来收集信息？ ·这些方法的利益是什么？ ·这些方法的损失是什么？	
5. 选择和论证自己的观点： ·你认为这个问题应当如何解决？解释你的观点。	

LESSON 11
How Do Advances in Technology Threaten Privacy?

Purpose of Lesson

In this lesson you participate in a simulated congressional debate on a bill intended to protect the privacy of medical information, while allowing that information to be stored and transmitted on computers as part of a national health care system. When you have finished the lesson, you should be able to explain and evaluate different positions on the privacy issues this proposal raises. You also should be able to present and defend your position.

Terms to Know

data bank /retrieve

How do computers affect privacy?

Computers affect the lives of everyone in our society. People use computers not only to keep track of information, but also to increase efficiency. Computers are involved in almost everything we do:

• from the production of electricity to the production of textbooks

• from the use of telephones to the use of credit cards

• from the checkout line at the grocery store to the check-cashing line at the bank

But computers present problems for privacy in modem society because they can store information permanently and they can easily retrieve the stored information. Computers store such information as how much electricity and water you use each month, the amount of taxes you pay, your hair color, eye color, and whether you wear glasses. In fact, as you can see from the chart on this page, information about you that is stored in computers could draw a detailed picture of your life.

第十一课：科技进步如何对隐私产生威胁？

本课目标

在本课中，你们将进行一场模拟国会辩论并讨论一项法案：该法案要求保护医疗信息的隐私，同时又允许用计算机将这些医疗信息存储并传输到全国医疗保健系统中。学完本课后，你们应该能够解释和评估这项法案所提出的有关隐私问题的不同观点，你们也应该能够提出并论证你自己的观点。

掌握词汇

数据库　　　　　　　信息检索

电脑如何影响了隐私？

电脑影响着我们的社会中每个人的生活。人们使用电脑不仅用来掌握信息，也为了提高效率。几乎我们做的所有事当中都涉及到电脑：

- 从电力的产生到印制课本
- 从打电话到使用信用卡
- 从商店的收银机到银行的支票兑现系统

因为电脑可以永久存储信息，并且可以很轻易地对存储信息进行检索，因此现代社会中电脑给人们的隐私带来了许多问题。电脑里会存储你每个月用多少电和水、你所支付的税款数额、你的头发颜色、你眼睛的颜色或你是否戴眼镜。事实上，就像你们在本页图表中看到的一样，电脑中保存的所有关于你的个人信息，可以清晰具体地描绘出一幅有关你的生活的图景。

Although certain laws impose some restrictions, organizations usually can decide whether they will share the information they have stored in their computers, and several private companies have created large computer data banks by combining information from different sources, such as the forms people fill out when they apply for a loan, credit card, or driver's license. They sell this information to businesses that use it to identify people who might buy their products. Information disclosed to one person for one reason may be retrieved by other people and used for other purposes.

Computers make it almost impossible for individuals to control who learns personal information about them. As time goes by, computers will become more powerful; they will be able to store more information and retrieve it faster. More people and organizations will use computers, and privacy problems are likely to increase.

　　尽管某些法律对此有一定的限制，但某些机构还是可以自行决定是否要分享他们存储在电脑中的信息。一些私人企业通过整合不同来源的信息（例如人们在申请贷款、信用卡或驾驶执照时所填的表格），建立了庞大的电脑数据库。他们将这些信息出售给各企业，用于企业确认产品的消费人群（即谁会购买他们的产品）。出于某种原因透露给某个对象的信息，可能会被其他人检索到并用于其他目的。

　　电脑使个人几乎不可能掌控究竟是谁知道了自己的个人信息。随着时间的推移，电脑的威力变得越来越强大，人们将能在电脑中存储更多的信息，检索的速度也会越来越快。将会有更多的个人和公共机构使用电脑，隐私问题也可能会随之增加。

Information Stored in a Computer Data Bank	
Every Time You	**A Computer Stores**
use your telephone	the number you call, the date, and the length of time you talk
rent a movie from a video store	the name of that movie and the date you rented it
use a credit card	the date, amount of the purchase, name and location of the store, and a descriptionof what you bought
subscribe to a newspaper or magazine	your name and address, the name of the newspaper or magazine, and the dates your subscription starts and ends
apply for a loan	your address and telephone number, the name, address, and phone number of the place you work, how much money you earn, the value of the property you own, how much money you already owe, I and how much you pay on your debts each month
apply for car insurance	your address, driving record, the make and model of your car, how far you drive to work, and how far you drive each year
pay your bills	the date and amount of your payment

电脑数据库中存储的信息	
每次当你	一部电脑将存储
拨打电话时	你呼叫的号码、打电话的日期和时间长度
从一家录像带店租一部电影碟片时	那部电影的名字和你租碟的时间
用你的信用卡刷卡消费时	你购买物品的时间和数额、商店的名字和地点、你购买的物品的描述
订阅报纸或杂志时	你的名字和住址、报纸或杂志的名字、订阅的起始时间？
申请贷款	你的住址和电话；你工作单位的名称、地址和电话号码；你挣了多少钱；你所拥有的财产价值；你已经欠了多少钱；每个月你将偿还多少债务？
申请汽车保险	你的住址、驾驶记录、你的汽车的品牌和型号、你驾车去上班的距离、每年你驾车的里程是多少
支付帐单时	支付的时间和数额

What do you think?

1. Do you think computers pose a serious problem for people who want to maintain their privacy? Why or why not?

2. Do you think the advantages of computer technology outweigh the privacy problems they create? Explain your position.

3. What measures, if any, would you support to prevent private companies from compiling and storing data about the private activities of individuals?

4. How could individuals act in order to limit the ability of private companies to gather and store information about their activities?

How does technology affect privacy in health care?

Since the ancient days of Hippocrates, people have expected their doctors to keep their medical condition confidential. The concern for privacy of medical information derives in part from its personal nature, and in part from the way it can reveal our weaknesses and make us vulnerable. The doctor's obligation of confidentiality promotes health care by encouraging us to report our symptoms to our physician without fear of embarrassment. Today, that confidentiality is not only a doctor's moral obligation but his or her legal obligation as well.

Nevertheless, the privacy of medical information is far from absolute. To provide insurance benefits, health insurance companies require covered patients to consent to their doctor's disclosure of their medical condition. Even people without insurance may be required to permit their doctors to disclose their medical condition, for example if that condition is an issue in a lawsuit. Public health concerns have led to laws requiring doctors to report medical information regarding their patients to government health agencies, such as when the information is needed to prevent the spread of infectious diseases.

Now, however, new concerns have been raised about the privacy of medical information. These concerns arise from two factors.

• The widespread use of health insurance to pay for medical care has resulted in the creation of computer files and data banks that store medical information regarding identifiable individuals.

• A national health care program has been proposed that would require patients to present a "National Health Card" before receiving treatment. The card would make more medical information available systematically. In particular, if smart cards with magnetic strips were used for this purpose, the National Health Card could contain an individual's entire medical history.

你怎么看?

1. 电脑是不是给那些想要保护自己隐私的人带来了很严重的问题? 为什么? 为什么不?

2. 电脑技术的优势是否大于它们所产生的隐私问题? 解释你的观点。

3. 你会采取什么措施(如果有的话)来阻止私人企业收集和存储有关个人隐私活动的信息?

4. 针对私人企业收集和存储个人隐私活动信息的能力,个人可以通过什么行动对此加以限制?

技术如何影响医疗隐私?

从希波克拉底的古希腊时代开始,人们就希望医生能对自己的健康状况保密。对医疗信息隐私的关注,部分源于医疗信息本身的特性,也有部分是因为它以某种方式暴露了我们的弱点以及我们容易受到伤害的地方。医生的保密义务使我们不再害怕尴尬而将自己的病症告诉医生。今天,保密不仅是医生的道德义务,也是他或她的法律义务。

然而,医疗信息的隐私性并不是完全绝对的。为了提供保险福利,医疗保险公司要求病人同意医生披露他们的健康状况。即使没有买保险的人,也可能会被要求允许医生透露其治疗情况,比如在有关医疗条件的诉讼中。对公共健康的关注也促使法律要求医生将病人的相关医疗信息向政府卫生机构报告,例如政府为了防止传染病的蔓延就需要类似的信息。

然而,有关医疗信息的隐私,人们现在又有了新的关注点,这些关注主要来源于以下两个因素:

- 用于支付医疗保健费用的医疗保险的广泛应用,促进了存储着可识别的个人医疗信息的电脑文件及数据库的建立。

- 全民卫生保健计划的提出,要求病人在接受治疗前出示"国民健康卡"。该卡将能提供更系统的医疗信息。特别是,如果启用了带有磁条的智能卡,"国民健康卡"中将会容纳个人的全部医疗记录。

Critical Thinking Exercise

USING INTELLECTUAL TOOLS TO EVALUATE, TAKE, AND DEFEND A POSITION

Work with a study partner or in small groups to answer the following questions about the privacy problems that would be created by the National Health Card proposal described below. Be prepared to share your answers with the class.

Imagine that you are a member of the United States House of Representatives. Legislation has been proposed that would require every individual to present his or her National Health Card in order to receive medical care. Doctors and hospitals will be able to access the individual's entire medical history with the card; the information will be stored on the card's magnetic strip. Whenever medical care is provided, the information on the card will be updated. The government will assume the responsibility of paying for medical care; information about services provided will be forwarded electronically and stored in the government's central computer data bank, and all paperwork will be eliminated.

I. Identify the person claiming privacy.

• Whose claim to privacy would be endangered by the use of a National Health Card?

• What medical information might people not want to have in a government data bank? Why?

• How could information about individuals be kept private?

2. Identify the person wishing to limit or invade the other's privacy.

• How might a National Health Card limit or invade people's privacy?

• Why might the federal government wish to have people use a National Health Card?

3. Examine relevant considerations. create.

• By taking advantage of health insurance benefits from the government, do people consent to disclosure or use of information pertaining to their health care? Explain your position.

• Do you think the federal government has a legal right to require the use of a National Health Card and to maintain medical information about people in a centralized computer data bank? Why or why not?

重点思考练习

运用知识工具评估、选择并论证某种观点

与一位同学一起或分成小组，合作回答下文中所描述的"国民健康卡"提案会产生的隐私问题。准备好向全班解释你们的答案。

想像一下，如果你是美国众议院的一位议员，一项提交到众议院待审议的立法提案中要求，每个人都要出示他或她的"国民健康卡"以便接受治疗。医生和医院将能够通过这张卡片获得个人的全部医疗记录，这些信息都储存在卡片上的磁条中，每次接受治疗时，卡上的信息将被更新。政府将承担支付医疗保健费用的责任，有关治疗的信息将被自动转发，并存储在政府的中央电脑数据库中，同时，所有的纸质档案将被淘汰。

1. 找出要求隐私的对象
   - 谁声称"国民健康卡"的使用使自己的隐私受到了威胁？
   - 人们不希望政府数据库里保存哪些医疗信息？为什么？
   - 如何能将个人信息保密？

2. 找出希望限制或侵犯他人隐私的对象
   - "国民健康卡"可能会怎样限制或侵犯人们的隐私？
   - 为什么联邦政府会希望人们使用"国民健康卡"？

3. 研究相关考虑因素
   - 通过享受政府的健康保险福利所带来的好处，民众是否同意披露或使用有关医疗护理的信息？解释你的观点。
   - 你认为联邦政府是否有合法权利要求人们使用"国民健康卡"，并且在中央电脑数据库中存储民众的医疗信息？为什么有？为什么没有？

- In your opinion, would requiring the use of a National Health Card violate a legal obligation of the federal government to respect the privacy of citizens? Explain your position.

- Do you think requiring the use of a National Health Card would violate a moral obligation of the federal government to respect the privacy of citizens? Explain your position.

4. Evaluate alternative solutions.

- What are the costs and benefits of the federal government requiring people to use a National Health Card?

- What are some means the federal government could use to ensure the privacy of medical information it collects? What are the benefits and costs of each of these means?

5. Take and defend a position.

- What position would you take on requiring the use of a National Health Card? Explain your reasoning.

Critical Thinking Exercise

EVALUATING, TAKING, AND DEFENDING A POSITION ON A NATIONAL HEALTH CARD

During this activity, you participate in a simulated congressional hearing. You suggest alternative ways of dealing with privacy issues raised by a National Health Card, Your teacher will, divide your class into the following groups:

- **Doctors United for Health Care**. Your group is in favor of a national health care program and strongly supports any plan that would do away with paperwork. You believe the benefits of the National Health Card outweigh the privacy problems it would requirements on the government to protect privacy, you do not believe any such requirements should be imposed on medical care providers, because they are not needed.

- **Citizens for Efficiency in Health Care**. Your group favors any proposal that it believes will improve government health care programs and make them more efficient. To gain support for the National Health Card proposal, you are willing to propose that severe penalties be imposed on doctors, hospitals, and the government for unauthorized or improper use or disclosure of medical information.

· 在你看来，联邦政府要求人们使用"国民健康卡"是否违反了政府尊重公民隐私权的法律义务？解释你的观点。

· 你是否认为联邦政府要求使用"国民健康卡"违反了政府尊重公民隐私权的道德义务？解释你的观点。

4. 评估备选解决方案

· 联邦政府要求人们使用"国民健康卡"的利弊得失是什么？

· 联邦政府可以运用哪些方法来保护它所收集的医疗信息的隐私？

· 这些方法都各有什么利弊得失？

5. 选择和论证自己的观点

· 关于政府对使用"国民健康卡"的要求，你会选择什么观点？说明你的理由。

重点思考练习

评估、选择和论证有关"国民健康卡"问题的观点

在本次练习中，针对"国民健康卡"产生的隐私问题，你们将参加一场模拟国会听证会，并提出一些备选解决方案。老师将会将你们班分成以下几组：

支持医疗保健的医生联盟。 你们组赞成政府提出的国民医疗保健计划，并坚决支持淘汰所有纸质医疗档案。你们组认为"国民健康卡"带来的好处大于它可能产生的隐私问题。虽然你们组不反对人们要求政府保护隐私，但你们认为不应当对医疗服务的提供者提出任何这样的要求，因为这些要求是不必要的。

支持医疗保健效率的公民。 你们组赞成任何可以改善政府的医疗保健计划并使之更有效率的提案。为了争取对"国民健康卡"提案的支持，你们组建议，对未经授权或不正当使用、泄露医疗信息的医生、医院和政府采取严厉的惩罚措施。

- **Citizens for Privacy Committee.** Your group believes that the National Health Card proposal should be opposed unless safeguards, restrictions, and penalties are enacted that would provide real protection for the privacy of medical information.

- **People United against Tyranny.** Your group thinks it would be a dangerous mistake to allow the government to have access to each citizen's medical information, regardless of the legal restrictions that might be imposed to prevent misuse of that information. You oppose the National Health Card proposal under all circumstances.

- **House Information Subcommittee.** You will decide whether to approve the use of a National Health Card as part of a national health care program and whether to enact any special provisions to secure the privacy of medical information. You will listen to all views because you want to make the best possible decision. You know your constituents are concerned about and want health care, but they also value their privacy and freedom.

Preparing and Conducting the Hearing

The first four groups should prepare arguments supporting or opposing the use of a National Health Card, and suggest how (if at all) privacy of medical information could be preserved if such cards were used. The arguments should identify and take into account the benefits and costs of a National Health Card and the benefits and costs of the privacy-securing suggestions. The arguments also should explain how the group's position would

- protect the privacy of people
- give government a way of obtaining and using needed information to run a national health care program

The first four groups should select two or three spokespersons to present their arguments to the House Information Subcommittee. While the first four groups develop their arguments, the subcommittee should prepare questions to ask each group's spokespersons. The subcommittee also should elect a chairperson to conduct the hearing.

After the four groups have presented their arguments, each member of the subcommittee should express and explain his or her views on the creation of a National Health Card and on the privacy-securing suggestions that were made.

　　支持隐私的公民委员会。你们组认为，除非那些能真正起到保护医疗信息隐私作用的保障、限制和处罚措施能得以实施，否则就应当反对"国民健康卡"提案。

　　反对暴政的人民联盟。你们组认为，如果允许政府获取每个公民的医疗信息，这将是一个危险的错误，即便政府为防止滥用医疗信息会实施某些法律限制。你们组反对在任何情况下实施国民健康卡计划。

　　众议院信息小组委员会。你们组将决定是否批准作为国民医疗保健计划一部分的"国民健康卡"提案，以及是否要制定特定法规来保护医疗信息的隐私。你们组要为做出最好的决定而听取各方面的意见。你们知道，自己的选民在关注和期待医疗保健计划的同时也珍惜自己的隐私和自由。

准备和举行听证会

　　上述分组说明中的前四组应准备论据来支持或反对使用"国民健康卡"，并针对"国民健康卡"（如果该计划得以通过）应当如何保护医疗信息的隐私提出自己的建议。各组所使用的论据应当明确并考虑到使用"国民健康卡"的利弊得失，以及各组提出的有关隐私保护的建议所带来的利弊得失。同时，各组使用的论据还应当说明自己的建议将会如何：

- 保护人们的隐私
- 为政府提供一种获取和使用必要信息的方式，以便实施国民医疗保健计划

　　前四组应选出两到三个发言人，向众议院信息小组委员会陈述各自的论点。在前四组准备各自的论据时，小组委员会应准备好要问各组发言人的问题。小组委员会也应选出一位主席来主持听证会。

　　四个小组陈述完各自论点后，小组委员会的每位成员都应该说明并解释自己对于"国民健康卡"提案的观点，以及对隐私保护问题的建议。

Using the Lesson

1. Imagine that Congress was considering a law that would require everyone to have an I.D. number. The number would be used whenever a person filled out an official form, such as a tax return, hospital admission form, or an application for a passport, driver's license, or government benefits. The number also would be used if the person received a traffic ticket or was arrested. What arguments could you make in favor of this law? What arguments could you make to oppose it? Which arguments do you think are the strongest? Why?

2. Why do you think individuals and groups are willing to testify at public hearings? Think about the groups who have just been represented at your mock congressional hearing.

3. What are the benefits of holding hearings on decisions the government will make? What are the costs? Should all government decisions be made only after hearings? Why or why not?

知识运用

1.　想象一下，国会正在审议一项法律，要求每个人都应当有自己的身份证号码。人们在填写正式表格时都会用到这个号码，例如填写纳税申报单、医院住院单，或是填表申请护照、驾照或政府补贴。如果一个人收到交通罚单或被拘捕时也要用到这个号码，你会用什么论据来支持这项法案？你会用什么论据来反对这项法案？哪一种论据你认为更有说服力？为什么？

2.　为什么你认为个人和团体都愿意在公开听证会上作证？试想一下在你们刚刚进行的模拟国会听证会上那些被代表的团体。

3.　政府对需要决策的问题举行听证会带来了什么利益？又会产生什么损失呢？所有政府的决定都只能在举行听证会之后做出吗？为什么？为什么不？

LESSON 12

What Privacy Rights Should People Have with Regard to Their Own Bodies?

Purpose of Lesson

This lesson examines the right of privacy a person has with regard to his or her own body. The lesson provides an opportunity for your class to conduct.a legislative hearing concerning the extent to which this right of privacy should be protected when the person's life is at stake. When you have completed this lesson, you should be able to evaluate, take, and defend positions on the issue of privacy it contains.

Term to Know

living wil

Critical Thinking Exercise

EXAMINING PRIVACY AND BODILY INTEGRITY

Your class will be divided into four groups to complete this exercise. Each group should read the selection assigned to it and answer the "What do you think?" questions. Be prepared to share your answers with the class.

Do you think people have especially strong privacy rights with regard to their own bodies?   ☞

第十二课：人们对自己的身体应当有什么隐私权利?

本课目标

　　本课研究一个人对他或她自己的身体所拥有的隐私权。你们全班将有机会举行一场模拟立法听证会，讨论当一个人的生命受到威胁时，隐私权应当得到保护的程度。学完本课后，你们应该能够评估、选择和论证本课所包含的隐私问题的观点。

掌握词汇

　　生前遗嘱

重点思考练习

研究隐私和身体的完整性

　　你们班将被分成四组来完成本次练习。每个小组应阅读各自的指定材料，并回答"你怎么看？"这一部分的问题。准备好与全班分享你们的答案。

你觉得人们对有关自己身体的事情拥有更多的隐私权吗?

1. Henning Jacobson did not want to be vaccinated against smallpox. The Cambridge Board of Health had determined that vaccination was needed to prevent the spread of the disease, and Massachusetts law required that Jacobson submit to the Board of Health's order or face a fine. Jacobson claimed the state had no power to compel him to be vaccinated; that "a compulsory vaccination law is unreasonable, arbitrary, and oppressive, therefore, hostile to the inherent right of every freeman to care for his own body and health in such way as to him seems best; and that the execution of such a law against one who objects to vaccination...is nothing short of an assault upon his person."

2. Antonio Rochin was sitting on the edge of his bed when three deputy sheriffs burst into his room. Spying two capsules on a night stand by the bed, the deputies demanded, "Whose stuff is this? Rochin grabbed the capsules and put them in his mouth. The three deputies jumped on him and tried to force him to open his mouth. Unable to do so, they handcuffed Rochin and took him to a hospital. There a doctor pumped Rochin's stomach by inserting a tube down his throat and forcing a liquid through the tube, making him vomit. The vomited capsules proved to contain morphine. Charged with possession of drugs, Rochin claimed the conduct of the deputies and the doctor and the bodily intrusion by which they accomplished the seizure of the capsules, violated his rights.

3. Rudolph Lee was brought to the emergency room by police. He had a gunshot wound to the left side of his chest, and the bullet was lodged under his collarbone. Lee told the police he had been shot by two robbers, but when they arrived at the hospital the police heard a different story: a shopkeeper who had been shot in an attempted robbery that night, and who had also shot his attacker, had been brought to the same emergency room; this shopkeeper identified Lee as the man who had tried to rob him. After an investigation, Lee was charged with attempted robbery, and the government sought a court order requiring Lee to submit to surgery to remove the bullet, so that the bullet could be examined to see if it was fired from the shopkeeper's gun. Lee refused to consent to the surgery, and argued that it would violate his constitutional rights to compel him to submit to such a procedure.

4. Elizabeth Bouvia wanted her nasogastric feeding tube removed. Against her will, doctors at the hospital had routed the tube through her nose and down her throat into her stomach in order to keep her alive. Cerebral palsy had rendered Elizabeth's arms and legs useless-she could not even sit up in bed. Unable to eat solid food at all, Elizabeth was spoon-fed a liquid-like diet but was not consuming enough to avoid starving.

1.　亨宁·雅各布森不想注射天花疫苗。剑桥地区卫生委员会规定，该地区所有人都需要接种该疫苗以防止疾病蔓延。同时马萨诸塞州法律规定，雅各布森必须服从剑桥地区卫生委员会的规定，否则将被处以罚款。雅各布森认为，州政府没有权力强迫他接种疫苗："这种强制接种疫苗的法规是不合理的、武断的和有强迫性的，以一种看上去对我最好的方式，实际上却侵犯了每个自由人生来就有的照顾自己身体和健康的权利，对一个拒绝接种疫苗的人强制执行这样的法律……简直就是一种人身攻击。"

2.　三名副警长闯进他的房间时，安东尼奥·罗钦正坐在他的床边。看到床头柜上两粒胶囊，警长们问："这是谁的东西？"罗钦抓起胶囊放进嘴里。警察们跳到他身上，试图强行掰开他的嘴却没有成功。他们给罗钦戴上手铐，将他带到医院。医生将一根导管插进了罗钦的喉咙，让药液顺着喉管流入他的胃里令他呕吐。事实证明，罗钦吐出来的胶囊中含有吗啡。罗钦被指控藏有毒品，但他认为警察和医生从他身体中获取胶囊的行为是对他身体的侵犯。

3.　鲁道夫·李被警察送进了急诊室。他的胸部左侧中枪，子弹从他的锁骨下射入。李先生告诉警方，有两名匪徒朝他开枪。但当他们到达医院后，警方却听到了另一个版本的故事：一个商店老板被企图抢劫的劫匪击中，店主自己开枪还击，并被送进了李先生所在的急诊室；店主随即认出了企图抢劫他的人就是李先生。经过调查，李先生被控图谋抢劫。政府请法院下令，要求李先生同意做手术取出子弹，以便检查这颗子弹是否是从店主的手枪中射出的。李先生拒绝接受手术，并认为法院迫使他服从这样的法律程序，将是对其宪法权利的侵犯。

4.　伊丽莎白·包维亚想拆掉她的鼻饲管。与她的意愿相反的是，医生们将鼻饲管从她的鼻子穿入经过喉咙直通到胃部，以维持她的生命。脑性麻痹（脑中风）已经使伊丽莎白的胳膊和腿丧失了功能，她甚至无法在床上坐起来。所有固体食物伊丽莎白都不能吃，而只能依靠护士用勺子喂服流食，但这样还是无法抵抗饥饿。

Her weight had dropped to 65 or 70 pounds when the hospital staff determined that feeding through a nasogastrictube was necessary to save her life. Now, through her lawyers, Elizabeth was asking the court to order the doctors to respect her wishes and remove the tube they had inserted over her objections, even if that meant she would starve to death in the immediate future, and even if, as her doctors claimed, she could live another 15 or 20 years with the feeding tube in place.

What do you think?

1. Who is claiming a right to privacy or bodily integrity in this situation? How is the person's privacy or bodily integrity being violated? How serious are the violations or intrusions?

2. Who is opposing or limiting the claim of privacy or bodily integrity? What are the reasons for opposing or limiting the claim of privacy or bodily integrity?

3. Are the intrusions on privacy or bodily integrity necessary, or are there other ways of managing the conflict?

4. Do you think there are sufficient grounds to invade the person's privacy and bodily integrity in this situation, considering the seriousness of the intrusion and the importance of the reasons for it? Explain your position.

What are reasonable legislative limits regarding bodily privacy?

As you have seen, individual interests in privacy and bodily integrity can come into conflict with the interests of society in a number of different contexts. The government may need to intrude on a person's privacy and bodily integrity in order to obtain evidence of a crime, in order to protect the public health and prevent the spread of disease, or in order to protect the health of the very person whose privacy and bodily integrity is invaded.

Reasonable people may have different opinions about how the privacy conflicts in these situations should be resolved. In each of these situations, some might think that the interests of society are more important than the privacy interests of the individual, some might think that the individual's interests are more important than the interests of society, and some might think that the particular facts of the situation in question must be evaluated to determine which interests are more important.

当她的体重下降到·65 到 70 磅时，医生们决定必须要用鼻饲管来拯救她的生命。现在，伊丽莎白通过她的律师请求法院下令，要求医生尊重她的个人意愿，摘除他们不顾她的反对而插入的鼻饲管，即便这将意味着她在不久的将来会因过度饥饿而死亡，即便医生们认为插入鼻饲管后她可以多活 15 到 20 年。

你怎么看？

1. 在上述材料中，谁在要求隐私权或身体完整性的权利？这个人的隐私或身体完整性遭到了怎样的侵犯？这种侵犯或妨碍有多严重？

2. 谁在反对或限制这个人对隐私或身体完整性的要求？为什么要反对或限制这种对隐私或身体完整性的要求？

3. 这种对隐私或身体完整性的侵犯是必要的吗？或者还有其他方式来解决冲突吗？

4. 在上述材料中，考虑到侵犯当事人的隐私和身体完整性的严重性，以及侵犯的理由的重要性，你认为是否有足够的理由这么做？解释你的观点。

对身体隐私来说什么样的法律限制是合理的？

正如你们所看到的，个人在隐私和身体完整性方面的权益在许多不同的情况下会与社会的其他利益发生冲突。政府可能要侵犯一个人的隐私和身体完整性，以便获取犯罪证据、保障公众健康、防止疾病传播，或者这么做是为了保障某个特殊对象的隐私和身体完整性不被侵犯。

针对在这些情况下该如何解决隐私冲突，理性的人会有不同的看法。以上每一种情况当中，都会有人认为社会利益要比个人隐私权重要，也会有人认为个人利益比社会利益更重要，还会有人认为在特定情况下必须先对具体事实进行评估，才能确定哪种利益更重要。

In the following exercise you will engage in a simulated legislative hearing on the topic of life-preserving medical care. The issue the state legislature must resolve is whether individuals should be free to refuse such care at all, and if so, under what circumstances. In order to address this issue, the state legislature has formed a special committee which will conduct a hearing and present its recommendations to the legislature.

Critical Thinking Exercise

EVALUATING, TAKING, AND DEFENDING A POSITION ON BODILY INTEGRITY

To conduct this activity, your class should be divided into the following groups:

• **Doctors for Ethical Health Care.** Your group is in favor of letting patients make their own decisions about medical treatment in most circumstances, but only when they are capable of giving informed consent. Your group is concerned that in many cases, a person with medical problems may refuse treatment because he or she is depressed, rather than making an informed, rational decision. Particularly when the medical treatment would or could prolong the person's life, refusal is contrary to the person's best interests, and may well reflect the influence of psychological depression.

• **Association of Health Insurers.** Your group believes that doctors often go too far in attempting to prolong an individual's life, expending vast efforts and resources with little hope of success. Your group supports broad protection of an individual's right to refuse medical treatment, even in circumstances when that treatment could be life-saving.

• **Confederation of Concerned Religious Leaders.** Your group believes that it is morally wrong for an individual to refuse life-saving medical treatment, except when that refusal is based on religious conviction, as in the case of Jehovah's Witnesses refusing blood transfusions. Your group contends that the state has an absolute duty to prevent suicide, and is determined not to allow an individual's claims to privacy and bodily integrity interfere with that duty.

在下面的练习中，你们将参加一场主题为"维持生命的医疗"的模拟立法听证会。州议会面临着一个急需解决的问题：个人是否可以自由地拒绝所有维持生命的医疗护理，如果可以，那么具体应当是在什么情况下。为了解决这一问题，州议会已经成立了一个特别委员会，并将举行一场听证会，听取相关提案的陈述。

重要思考练习

评估、选择和论证有关身体完整性的观点

为了进行此次练习，你们班应分为以下几组：

支持合乎道德的医疗的医生。你们组支持在大多数情况下让病人自行决定自己的治疗方案，但仅限于他们能够做出理性决定的时候。你们组关注的是，在许多案例中，病人可能会因为情绪低沉沮丧而拒绝接受治疗，做出了不明智和不理性的决定。特别是接受治疗是能够或可能延长病人生命的时候，如果拒绝接受治疗是违背了病人的最大利益的，并可能更多地是受到了心理抑郁的影响。

健康保险公司协会。你们组认为，医生往往在试图延长病人生命的事情上做得过多，消耗了巨大的努力和资源，成功的希望却不大。你们组支持更广泛地保护个人拒绝接受治疗的权利，即便是这种治疗可能会挽救生命。

相关宗教领袖联盟。你们组认为，个人拒绝维持生命的医护治疗在道德上是错误的，除非这种拒绝是基于某种宗教信仰，就像"耶和华见证人"（译者注：某种宗教团体）拒绝输血一样。你们组认为，州政府有绝对义务阻止人们自杀，因此你们决不允许任何个人对隐私和身体完整性的要求干扰这一义务的实现。

- **Advocates for the Elderly.** Your group thinks people should have the right to die with dignity, and that an individual's considered decision regarding medical treatment should be respected. However, your group is concerned that undue pressure might be placed on a person to refuse life-saving medical treatment, either by those who would gain financially by avoiding the cost of the treatment, or by those who are burdened by having to care for the person. Your group seeks to have the legislature approve the use of living wills, which provide clear evidence of an individual's wishes with regard to life-saving medical care, together with safeguards to ensure that the directions recorded in these documents are not influenced by undue pressure from others.

- **Committee on Life-Saving Medical Care.** You will decide whether individuals will be allowed to refuse life-saving medical care, and if so, under what circumstances. You will listen to all views because you want to make the best possible decision. You know your constituents value their privacy and freedom, but they also are concerned to protect and preserve the sanctity and value of human life, and to safeguard people from their own mistakes.

 How would you balance the privacy rights of patients with the concerns of society and the medical profession? ☞

老年人的支持者。你们组认为，人们应该有权利让自己死得有尊严。同时，对于是否接受医护治疗，经过深思熟虑的个人决定应当得到尊重。但你们组更关注的是，某些不正当的压力会导致当事人拒绝接受维持生命的治疗。这些压力要么来自于那些因为节省治疗费用而获得经济利益的人，或者来自于那些担负必须照顾病人责任的人。你们组试图促使州议会批准使用"生前遗嘱"，为个人有关维持生命的医疗问题上的意愿提供明确的证据，也确保这些文件中记录的决定并未受到来自他人的不正当的压力。

维持生命医疗委员会。你们组将决定是否允许个人拒绝接受维持生命的医疗，以及如果允许，那么应当是在什么特定情况下。你们会听取各方意见以便作出最好的、最可行的决定。你们应当了解，人们在珍惜自己的隐私和自由的同时，也关注保护和维系个人生命的尊严和价值，以及保护人们避免因为自己的错误而受损。

考虑到社会和医学界的关注，你会如何权衡病人的隐私权？

Conducting the Hearing

The first four groups should prepare proposals specifying the circumstances, if any, in which a person may refuse life-saving medical care. These groups should also prepare arguments to support their proposals, explaining how their group's position would balance

• the individual's interest in privacy and bodily integrity.

• society's interests in preserving life, in preventing suicide, in maintaining the ethics of the medical profession, and in ensuring that any decision to refuse life-saving medical care will be carefully considered and will be made without undue pressure.

The first four groups should select two or three spokespersons to present their proposals and arguments to the Committee on Life-Saving Medical Care. While the first four groups are working on their arguments, the committee should prepare questions to ask each group's spokespersons, and select a chairperson to conduct the hearing. The committee should review the chart on page 142,144 in preparing its questions.

After the four groups have presented their proposals and arguments, each member of the committee should express and explain his or her views on the circumstances, if any, in which individuals should be free to refuse life-saving medical care. The class as a whole should then conclude the activity by voting on the various proposals that were presented.

Using the Lesson

1. Should it make any difference whether a person's refusal of life-saving medical care is based on his or her religious convictions? Do research to find out how courts have dealt with efforts by Jehovah's Witnesses to refuse blood transfusions for themselves and for their children. Give a report to your class on what you learn, and explain your own views on this issue.

2. Should the government be permitted to require a person to receive mental health treatment? Under what circumstances? What forms of mental health treatment should the government be able to compel a person to receive? Can the government compel a person to take medications for mental illness? To engage in psychotherapy sessions? To submit to brain surgery? Do research to learn about your state's laws on involuntary commitment of persons for mental health treatment. Write a letter to the editor or to your state legislators expressing your views on this topic.

举行听证会

前四个小组应当根据指定的背景材料准备提案（如果有的话），在指定的背景材料中，人们可以拒绝维持生命的医疗服务。各小组也应当准备论据来支持自己的提案，说明自己的观点将如何平衡以下各项之间的关系：

个人利益：有关隐私和身体完整性的。

社会利益：有关维持生命、阻止自杀、维护医学界伦理，并确保任何拒绝接受维持生命的医疗的决定是经过慎重考虑的、也没有受到不正当压力的。

前四个小组应选择两个或三个发言人向"维持生命医疗委员会"陈述各自的提案和论据。在前四个组的工作准备论据的时候，委员会小组应准备要问每个小组发言人的问题，并选出一位主持人进行听证会。委员会小组应当在准备问题的时候仔细阅读第143、145页的图表。

前四个小组陈述完各自的提案和论据后，委员会小组的每位成员都应该陈述和说明他或她有关背景材料的看法；在这一背景材料（如果有的话）中，个人可以自由地拒绝维持生命的医疗服务。全班应当一起总结此次听证会，并对各组公开陈述的提案进行投票表决。

知识运用

1. 如果一个人拒绝维持生命的医疗服务是基于他或她的宗教信仰，这是否会带来一些影响？调查并了解法院是如何处理"耶和华见证人"（某宗教团体）拒绝为自己和子女输血的案例的。向全班报告你所了解的内容，并解释自己对这个问题的看法。

2. 是否应当允许政府要求人们接受心理治疗？在什么情况下允许政府这么做？ 政府能迫使个人接受哪种形式的心理治疗？政府能不能迫使个人接受精神病药物治疗？或者参加心理辅导？动脑部手术？调查并了解你们州的法律中有关非个人自愿接受心理治疗的条款。写一封信给编辑或州议员就这个问题说说你的看法。

LESSON 13

How Should We Resolve Conflicts between Privacy and Freedom of the Press?

Purpose of Lesson

This final lesson on privacy provides an opportunity to examine issues that arise from the activities of the press. Your class will discuss these issues and establish guidelines for members of the press to follow when they investigate and report on private citizens.

When you have finished the lesson, you should be able to explain and evaluate different positions on this issue. You also should be able to explain the usefulness of establishing a policy to deal with situations that are likely to arise again and again.

Terms to Know

common law

libel

slander

What privacy boundaries should be respected by the press?

The First Amendment provides that "Congress shall make no law...abridging the freedom... of the press." But under the common law, members of the press, like others, have been held liable for damages when they libel or slander someone by publishing or broadcasting false statements that injure the person's reputation. If the damaging statements are true, however, no suit for libel or slander can be maintained.

Does this mean the press is free to invade our privacy and publish the most private and intimate facts of our lives? Are there boundaries of privacy that journalists must respect? Are there some topics that should be considered off-limits?

第十三课：我们应当如何解决隐私和新闻自由之间的冲突？

本课目标

在这节关于隐私的最后一课中，你们将有机会研究新闻媒体的活动中产生的隐私问题。你们将针对这些问题进行讨论，并为媒体从业人员制定一套行为准则，以便他们在采访和报道普通公民时可以参考。

学完本课后，你们应该能够解释和评估有关这一问题的不同观点。针对某些可能重复出现的隐私问题，你们也应该能够解释制定一项政策在处理这类问题方面的实用性。

掌握词汇

　　普通法

　　诽谤

　　造谣

新闻媒体应当尊重什么样的隐私界限？

联邦宪法第一修正案规定："国会不得制定法律剥夺言论自由或出版自由"。但根据普通法，新闻媒体的从业人员同其他人一样，也要为他们诽谤或造谣他人时所造成的伤害负责，当他们通过出版或广播发表伤害当事人名誉的虚假报道时。但如果这种破坏性的报道是真实的，就无法起诉他们恶意诽谤或造谣了。

那么，这是否意味着媒体可以自由地侵犯我们的隐私，并公开那些我们生活中最私密的事情？新闻工作者是否必须尊重隐私权的界限？是否有一些事情应该被视为不可触碰的禁区？

What about the means used by journalists to investigate their subjects? Can reporters use hidden cameras and microphones to record the people they are investigating? Can they lie about their identity to get people to reveal things they would not tell a reporter? Can they search a person's garbage to gather information?

Both of these types of issues-limits on the topics reporters choose to investigate, and limits on the ways they investigate their topics-can have significant impacts on the extent of privacy we enjoy in this country. These issues also involve other values, such as freedom and human dignity. The following exercise gives you an opportunity to explore the first type of issue: what limits there ought to be on the topics reporters choose to cover. Later, your class will have a chance to formulate guidelines for reporters to follow with regard to both types of issues.

 Do you think there are some people or subjects that should be off limits to reporters and the media?

☞ _____

　　那么对记者调查报道主题的方式有限制吗？记者可以使用隐藏摄像机和麦克风拍下他们正在调查采访的人吗？他们可以隐瞒自己的身份，让人们说出那些本来不会跟记者说的话吗？他们能不能在采访对象的垃圾中收集信息？

　　以下两种问题——对记者选择调查的主题的限制、对记者调查这些主题的方式的限制，会对我们在美国享有的隐私的程度产生很重要的影响。这些问题还涉及到诸如自由和人类尊严等其他价值。接下来的练习中，你们将有机会，探讨第一种问题：对记者选择报道的主题应当有什么限制。接下来，你们班将有机会制订出一份指南，以便让媒体记者在这两种问题上参考并遵守。

你认为是否有一些人和主题是记者和媒体所不能报道的？

Critical Thinking Exercise

EXAMINING INVASION OF PRIVACY BY THE PRESS

Read the following selection carefully. Then work with a study partner to complete the intellectual tool chart on page 142,144. Be prepared to explain your position to your class.

Briscoe v. Reader's Digest Association

In the late 1960s, Reader's Digest published an article titled 'The Big Business of Hijacking." One sentence in the article referred to Marvin Briscoe: "Typical of many beginners, Marvin Briscoe [and another man] stole a 'valuable-looking' truck in Danville, Ky., and then fought a gun battle with the local police, only to learn that they had hijacked four bowling-pin spotters." In fact, the theft had occurred in 1956, some eleven years before the article was published, and Mr. Briscoe had paid his debt to society and lived a crime-free life since then.

Mr. Briscoe sued for invasion of privacy, asserting that Reader's Digest's publication of "truthful but embarrassing private facts about his past life was wrongful." He claimed that he had assumed a place in respectable society and made many friends who were not aware of the incident in his earlier life; that these friends and his own 11-year-old daughter first learned of the incident as a result of the publication of the article, and that he had been humiliated and subjected to contempt and ridicule as a result.

In discussing Mr. Briscoe's claim, the California Supreme Court noted that

In many respects a person had less privacy in the small community of the 18th century than he did in the urbanizing late 19th century or he does today in the modem metropolis. Extended family networks, primary group relationships, and rigid communal mores served to expose an individual's every deviation from the norm and to straitjacket him in a vise of backyard gossip. Yet [it is] mass exposure to public gaze, as opposed to backyard gossip, which threaten[s] to deprive men of the right of scratching wherever one itches'.

Acceptance of the right to privacy has grown with the increasing capability of the mass media and electronic devices with their capacity to destroy an individual's anonymity, intrude upon his most intimate activities, and expose his most personal characteristics to public gaze... Men fear exposure not only to those closest to them....

重点思考练习

研究新闻媒体对隐私的侵犯

仔细阅读下文，然后与一位同学一起完成第 143、145 页的知识工具图表。准备好向全班解释你们的观点。

布里斯科诉读者文摘协会公司案

20 世纪 60 年代末，《读者文摘》发表了一篇名为《抢劫的大生意》的文章。文章中有一句话提到了马文·布里斯科："像很多新手一样，马文·布里斯科（和另一名男子）在肯塔基州的丹维尔偷了一辆"看上去很贵"的卡车，后来还与当地警察打了一场枪战，结果没想到他们还劫持了 4 个保龄球馆的球童。"事实上，这桩盗窃案发生在 1956 年，是这篇文章发表的 11 年前，而布里斯科先生已经向社会还清了债务，并且自从那时起就没再犯过罪。

布利斯科先生控告杂志社侵犯了他的隐私权，声称《读者文摘》刊登了他"真实却令人尴尬的过往生活是不对的。"他认为自己已经拥有了令人尊敬的社会地位，现在交往的朋友大多不知道他早年生活中发生的事；正是因为杂志刊登了这篇文章，这些朋友还有他 11 岁的女儿都是第一次知道此事，他也因此受到了他们的侮辱、蔑视和嘲笑。

在对布里斯科先生的起诉进行讨论时，加利福尼亚州最高法院指出：

比起 20 世纪的城市居民来说，生活在 19 世纪小社区当中的人们在许多方面都没什么隐私。扩大的家庭网络、主要的团体关系、僵化的公共道德观念都会曝光一个人每一次偏离规范的行为，并使他置身于"后院八卦"的包围之中。然而，（本案）使当事人的行为完全暴露在公众目光之下，可不仅仅是威胁要剥夺当事人"挠痒"权利的"后院八卦"。

现在，已经有越来越多的人承认个人的隐私权，与此同时，大众媒体和电子仪器也越来越有能力摧毁个人的匿名权、侵入个人最私密的活动、曝光个人最隐私的特征，并将这些都通通暴露在公众面前……人们害怕的是曝光的对象不仅仅是那些最亲近的人……

The claim is not so much one of total secrecy as it is of the right to define one's circle of intimacy....

On the other hand, the court also noted that

The right to keep information private [is] bound to clash with the right to disseminate information to the public.... [M] en are curious about the inner sanctums of their neighbors; the public will create its heroes and villains.... The masks we wear may be stripped away upon the occurrence of some event of public interest. ... the risk of exposure is a concomitant of urban life .... In a nation built upon the free dissemination of ideas, it is always difficult to declare that something may not be published.

Critical Thinking Exercise

IDENTIFYING GUIDELINES FOR REPORTERS

Your class should be divided into small groups to complete this exercise. Each group will be assigned to represent one of the following organizations:

- **Association of Responsible Newspaper Editors:** Your views are summarized by the motto of The New York Times: All the News That's Fit to Print.

- **Broadcast Entertainment Group:** Your views might be summarized as All the News That Fits, We Print.

- **People for Protection of Privacy:** Your group seeks strong protection for the privacy rights of private citizens.

- **First Amendment Foundation:** Your group stresses the importance of a free press to a free society, and the need to permit unrestricted discussion of any matter having any importance to the public.

- **Citizens for Decency and Dignity:** Your group opposes the lack of standards of decency and decorum in the press, particularly on television, and believes that the failure of mass media to govern itself responsibly justifies the imposition of standards of decency by the government.

Each group should develop a proposed policy or set of guidelines that addresses the following two issues:

- What limits should apply to the means used by journalists to investigate their subjects?

（人们）要求的并不是完全保密的隐私，而是一种定义自己的私密圈的权利……

另一方面，法院也指出：

"对个人信息保密的权利注定要与向公众传播信息的权利发生冲突……人们发自内心地对他们的邻居感到好奇。公众会虚构出自己心中的英雄和恶棍……在某些有关公共利益的事情发生时我们的面具被撕了下来……曝光的风险是城市生活的附属品……在一个在思想自由传播基础上建立的国家里，要求某些事不能被公开通常是很困难的。"

重点思考练习

明确记者的规范

全班将被分成小组完成本次练习。每个小组分别代表以下组织：

负责任的报纸编辑组成的联盟：你们组的观点可以用《纽约时报》的信条来概括：刊登一切可以印刷的新闻。

广播影视集团：你们组的观点可以归纳为：我们刊登所有适当的新闻。

支持隐私保护的人们：你们组旨在为公民个人的隐私权利寻求强有力的保障。

第一修正案基金会：你们组强调新闻自由对于自由社会的重要性，要允许对公众有任何重要性的任何问题进行无限制的讨论。

要求体面和尊严的公民：你们组反对缺乏行为准则和礼仪标准的新闻媒体，特别是电视媒体，并认为大众传媒缺乏负责任的自我管理证明了政府对媒体实施"正当准则"是必要的。

每个小组应制定一项政策提案或一套行为准则，用来解决以下两个问题：

应当对记者对报道主题进行调查时所使用的方法施加什么限制？

• What limits should apply to the topics journalists choose to investigate and report?

Each group should select two or three spokespersons to present each component of its proposed guidelines to the class. First, using a roundtable format, the groups should take turns presenting their views on what limits should apply to the topics journalists choose to investigate and report. Following discussion of this subject, the groups should take turns presenting their views on what limits should apply to the means used by journalists to investigate their subjects. The teacher should moderate the roundtable discussions. The class should conclude the activity by evaluating the usefulness of developing guidelines or policies to deal with privacy issues that are likely to arise again and again.

Using the Lesson

1. The film Absence of Malice presents a number of issues regarding the conduct of the press, including the propriety of a newspaper editor's decision to identify a source who was promised confidentiality. View the film and give a report to your class describing the issues it raises, and explain your position on these issues.

2. Some schools have used cameras to monitor hallways, outdoor campus areas, and problem classrooms. What do you think are the best arguments for and against this practice? Do you agree with the school's use of cameras in this way? Write a letter to the school board expressing your opinions.

3. Businesses such as banks and stores often have video cameras that tape persons doing business there. Make a chart of the costs and benefits of this practice. What alternatives can you think of for banks and stores to use? What are the costs and benefits of these alternatives? If you wanted to, how could you persuade the stores to stop using the cameras? Present your suggestions to the class.

应当对记者选择调查和报道的主题施加什么限制？

　　每个小组应选出两到三个发言人，负责向全班说明自己小组制定的行为准则的每个组成部分。首先，以圆桌会议的形式，对有关"应当如何限制记者选择调查和报道的主题"的问题陈述自己的观点。在讨论完这个问题后，接着各组应轮流陈述有关"应当如何限制记者对报道主题进行调查时所使用的方法"问题发表看法。老师应当引导圆桌讨论有序进行。全班应当总结此次活动，对制定准则或政策在解决可能重复出现的隐私问题上的作用进行评估。

知识运用

　　1. 电影《并无恶意》提出了一系列有关媒体行为的问题，包括一家报社的编辑决定找出某个他曾承诺要保密的信息来源的报料人。观看这部电影，向全班描述这部电影中提出的问题，并说明你对这些问题的看法。

　　2. 一些学校用摄像机监视学校的走廊、教室外的校园、以及很难管理的班级教室。你认为什么是支持或反对这种做法的最佳论据？你是否同意学校用这样的方式使用摄像机？给学校董事会写一封信，说明自己的看法。

　　3. 像银行、商店这样的地方通常都安装了摄像机，记录人们在那里所做的事情。针对这种做法，制作一个利弊得失的表格。你认为银行和商店还可以用其他什么方法？这些备选方案有哪些利弊得失？如果你希望说服银行和商店停止使用摄像机，你该怎么做？向全班说明你的建议。

附录1:
词汇表

common-law PL13. Relating to the body of law developed in England primarily from judicial decisions based on custom and precedent, unwritten in statute or code. The basis of the English legal system and of the system in all of the U.S. except Louisiana.

习惯法（《隐私》第十三课）：源自英国发展起来的法律体系，司法判定主要基于并未写入成文法令或条例的传统和判例。这是英国和美国联邦各州（除路易斯安那州外）法律体系的基础。

confidential PL2 (confidentiality). Told in secret; entrusted with private matters.

私密（《隐私》第二课）：被秘密告知的；被委托以私人事务。

conformity PL6. Action or behavior that is in accord with current rules, customs, or principles.

一致性（《隐私》第六课）：行为或举动与当前的规则、习俗或原则相一致。

consent PL9. Agreement as to action or opinion.

同意（《隐私》第九课）：对行为或观点的赞同。

creativity PL6. Originality; inventiveness.

创造力（《隐私》第六课）：独创性；发明创造的能力。

data bank PL11. A store of information.

数据库（《隐私》第十一课）：一种信息储存（系统）。

interest PL9. A right to or claim on something.

利益（《隐私》第九课）：对某事（物）的支配权或有权要求做某事得到某物。

effects PL9. Physical belongings.

财产（《隐私》第九课）：有形的所有物（财物）。

exclusion PL2. The act of keeping things private; keeping others out.

排斥（《隐私》第二课）：使事物（事情）保持私密的行为；将他人排除在外。

executive branch PL8. The branch of the government concerned with putting laws into effect.

行政部门（《隐私》第八课）：政府中主管有关法律付诸实行的部门。

factor PL4. Something that helps bring about a certain result.

因素（《隐私》第四课）：有助于带来某种结果的某事。

Freedom of Information Act PL9. A law passed by Congress in 1966 that gives people a legal right to documents from the federal government, unless the documents contain certain types of confidential or classified information.

信息自由法（《隐私》第九课）：1966年美国国会通过了该法案，赋予了美国人民获得联邦政府文件的合法权利，除非这些文件中包含了某些类型的秘密或机密信息。

hearsay PL7. Information or news heard from another person; rumor.

谣言（《隐私》第七课）：从他人处听说的消息或新闻；传闻。

injunction PL8. A court order prohibiting or requiring a specific course of action.

禁制令（《隐私》第八课）：禁止或规定某一具体行动计划的法令。

institution PL3. An established practice, custom, or pattern of behavior important in the cultural life of a society.

公共机构（《隐私》第三课）：在某一社会的文化生活中具有重要意义的一套既定的实践、习俗或行为模式。

intellectual stimulation PL6. Increased use of the intellect.

智力刺激（《隐私》第六课）：增进脑力的运用。

isolation PL2. The condition of being separate, alone, or free from external influence.

隔离（《隐私》第二课）：（处于）隔开的、单独的、或不受外界干扰的状态。

legality PL9. The fact of being lawful.

合法性（《隐私》第九课）：（是）合法的事实。

legal obligation PL9. A responsibility imposed by law.

法律义务（《隐私》第九课）：由法律规定的责任。

此处修改译文（原译为"责任"）：P33第九课掌握词汇、P28第七课第四行"波考认为道德义务应优先于法律义务"

libel PL13. A written or printed statement that unjustly damages a person's reputation or exposes him or her to ridicule.

诽谤（《隐私》第十三课）：不正义地伤害了某人的名誉，或使他（她）遭受他人嘲笑和侮辱的书面或印刷文书及陈述。

living will PL12. To make one's wishes known in advance in case a life threatening illness or accident should occur that renders one mentally incapacitated.

生前遗嘱（《隐私》第十二课）：提前公开某人的遗嘱，以防出现某种威胁生命的疾病或发生事故使立嘱人精神上失去行为能力。

loitering PL10. To stand around idly; to linger with no apparent purpose.

逗留（《隐私》第十课）：百无聊赖地站着；没有目的地闲晃。

moral obligation PL9. A duty arising from the inner sense of right or wrong.

道德义务（《隐私》第九课）：源于（人们）内心的是非观念而产生的责任和义务。

occupation PL4. A means of making a living; a profession or job.

职业（《隐私》第四课）：一种维持生计的方式；一种行业或工作。

privacy PL1. A condition of isolation, secrecy, or being apart from others.

隐私（《隐私》第一课）：隔离、隐秘或远离他人的状况。

prior restraint PL8. A hold or check that preceded an act or event.

预先制止令（《隐私》第八课）：在某项行动或事件发生前制止或阻止。（译者注：司法上预先禁止公布某项陈述或表达意见）

retrieve PL11. To locate data or information in a file, library, etc. and make it available for use, especially by means of computer.

信息检索（《隐私》第十一课）：特指运用电脑，在文件、图书馆等当中找出数据或信息的位置，并使之可用。

role PL4. The proper function of a person; characteristics and expected behavior of individuals.

角色（《隐私》第四课）：一个人的特定职责；个人的特性和预期行为。

secrecy PL2. Concealment.

隐秘（《隐私》第二课）：隐藏、隐蔽。

seizure PL9. Amendment IV of the Bill of Rights prohibits "unreasonable searches and seizures" by the government; the act or process of taking forcibly.

扣押（《隐私》第九课）：美国宪法第四修正案（权利法案）禁止政府对公民进行"无理的搜查和扣押"；强行拿取的行为或过程。

slander PL13. A false statement spoken maliciously to damage a person's reputation.

造谣（《隐私》第十三课）：为诋毁一个人的名誉而在口头上蓄意编造的虚假证词。

solitude PL1. The state of being alone.

孤独（《隐私》第一课）：独自一人的状态（独处）。

totalitarianism PL6 (totalitarian). A form of government in which one party exercises absolute control over all spheres of human life and opposing parties are not allowed to exist.

极权主义（《隐私》第六课）：某种政府形式中只有一个政党对人们生活的所有领域行使绝对的控制权，同时不允许其他反对党的存在。

value PL4/PL9. A principle, standard, or quality considered worthwhile or desirable.

价值观（《隐私》第四课、第九课）：被认为是有价值的或理想的准则、标准或品质。

warrant PL9. Amendment IV of the Bill of Rights. Evidence for or token of authority which grants the state the right to search and seizure, a warrant cannot be issued without the state first establishing probable cause-that is, reason to suspect that a crime has been committed.

授权（《隐私》第九课）：来源于美国联邦宪法第四修正案。授予国家搜查和扣押权利的权威的依据或象征；在国家没有事先提出合理根据（即怀疑罪案已经发生的理由）的前提下无法颁发准许搜查的法令（搜查令）。

writs of Assistance PL6. Before the American Revolution, English officials in the colonies used general search warrants, called Writs of Assistance, to enter the colonists' homes at any time and search them for evidence of crimes.

协查令（《隐私》第六课）：美国独立战争前，殖民地的英国官员使用一种叫做"协查令"的一般搜查令，这样他们可以随时进入殖民地居民的家中，搜寻他们的犯罪证据。

附录2：

The Constitution of the United States

We the People of the United States, in[注] Order to form a more perfect Union, establish Justice, insure domestic Tranquility, provide for the common defence, promote the general Welfare, and secure the Blessings of Liberty to ourselves and our Posterity, do ordain and establish this Constitution for the United States of America.

Article. I.

Section. 1   All legislative Powers herein granted shall be vested in a Congress of the United States, which shall consist of a Senate and House of Representatives.

Section. 2   The House of Representatives shall be composed of Members chosen every second Year by the People of the several States, and the Electors in each State shall have the Qualifications requisite for Electors of the most numerous Branch of the State Legislature.

No Person shall be a Representative who shall not have attained to the Age of twenty five Years, and been seven Years a Citizen of the United States, and who shall not, when elected, be an Inhabitant of that State in which he shall be chosen.

Representatives and direct Taxes shall be apportioned among the several States which may be included within this Union, according to their respective Numbers, which shall be determined by adding to the whole Number of free Persons, including those bound to Service for a Term of Years, and excluding Indians not taxed, three fifths of all other Persons. The actual Enumeration shall be made within three Years after the first Meeting of the Congress of the United States, and within every subsequent Term of ten Years, in such Manner as they shall by Law direct. The Number of Representatives shall not exceed one for every thirty Thousand, but each State shall have at Least one Representative; and until

---

注：原文：美国国家档案馆

  http://www.archives.gov/exhibits/charters/constitution_transcript.html

美利坚合众国宪法

我们合众国人民，为建立更完善的联邦，树立正义，保障国内安宁，提供共同防务，促进公共福利，并使我们自己和后代得享自由的幸福，特为美利坚合众国制定本宪法。

第一条

第一款　本宪法授予的全部立法权，属于由参议院和众议院组成的合众国国会。

第二款　众议院由各州人民每两年选举产生的众议员组成。每个州的选举人须具备该州州议会人数最多一院选举人所必需的资格。

凡年龄不满二十五岁，成为合众国公民不满七年，在一州当选时不是该州居民者，不得担任众议员。

［众议员名额和直接税税额，在本联邦可包括的各州中，按照各自人口比例进行分配。各州人口数，按自由人总数加上所有其他人口的五分之三予以确定。自由人总数包括必须服一定年限劳役的人，但不包括未被征税的印第安人。］ ①人口的实际统计在合众国国会第一次会议后三年内和此后每十年内，依法律规定的方式进行。每三万人选出的众议员人数不得超过一名，但每州至少须有一名众议员；在进行上述人口统计以前，新罕布什尔州有权选出三名，马萨诸塞州八名，罗得岛州和普罗维登斯种植地一名，康涅狄格州五名，纽约州六名，新泽西州四名，宾夕法尼亚州八名，特拉华州一名，马里兰州六名，弗吉尼亚州十名，北卡罗来纳州五名，南卡罗来纳州五名，佐治亚州三名。

such enumeration shall be made, the State of New Hampshire shall be entitled to chuse three, Massachusetts eight, Rhode-Island and Providence Plantations one, Connecticut five, New-York six, New Jersey four, Pennsylvania eight, Delaware one, Maryland six, Virginia ten, North Carolina five, South Carolina five, and Georgia three.

When vacancies happen in the Representation from any State, the Executive Authority thereof shall issue Writs of Election to fill such Vacancies.

The House of Representatives shall chuse their Speaker and other Officers; and shall have the sole Power of Impeachment.

Section. 3   The Senate of the United States shall be composed of two Senators from each State, chosen by the Legislature thereof for six Years; and each Senator shall have one Vote.

Immediately after they shall be assembled in Consequence of the first Election, they shall be divided as equally as may be into three Classes. The Seats of the Senators of the first Class shall be vacated at the Expiration of the second Year, of the second Class at the Expiration of the fourth Year, and of the third Class at the Expiration of the sixth Year, so that one third may be chosen every second Year; and if Vacancies happen by Resignation, or otherwise, during the Recess of the Legislature of any State, the Executive thereof may make temporary Appointments until the next Meeting of the Legislature, which shall then fill such Vacancies.

No Person shall be a Senator who shall not have attained to the Age of thirty Years, and been nine Years a Citizen of the United States, and who shall not, when elected, be an Inhabitant of that State for which he shall be chosen.

The Vice President of the United States shall be President of the Senate, but shall have no Vote, unless they be equally divided.

The Senate shall chuse their other Officers, and also a President pro tempore, in the Absence of the Vice President, or when he shall exercise the Office of President of the United States.

The Senate shall have the sole Power to try all Impeachments. When sitting for that Purpose, they shall be on Oath or Affirmation. When the President of the United States is tried, the Chief Justice shall preside: And no Person shall be convicted without the Concurrence of two thirds of the Members present.

任何一州代表出现缺额时，该州行政当局应发布选举令，以填补此项缺额。

众议院选举本院议长和其他官员，并独自拥有弹劾权。

第三款　合众国参议院由［每州州议会选举的］②两名参议员组成，任期六年；每名参议员有一票表决权。

参议员在第一次选举后集会时，立即分为人数尽可能相等的三个组。第一组参议员席位在第二年年终空出，第二组参议员席位在第四年年终空出，第三组参议员席位在第六年年终空出，以便三分之一的参议员得每二年改选一次。［在任何一州州议会休会期间，如因辞职或其他原因而出现缺额时，该州行政长官在州议会下次集会填补此项缺额前，得任命临时参议员。］③

凡年龄不满三十岁，成为合众国公民不满九年，在一州当选时不是该州居民者，不得担任参议员。

合众国副总统任参议院议长，但除非参议员投票时赞成票和反对票相等，无表决权。

参议院选举本院其他官员，并在副总统缺席或行使合众国总统职权时，选举一名临时议长。

参议院独自拥有审判一切弹劾案的权力。为此目的而开庭时，全体参议员须宣誓或作代誓宣言。合众国总统受审时，最高法院首席大法官主持审判。无论何人，非经出席参议员三分之二的同意，不得被定罪。

Judgment in Cases of Impeachment shall not extend further than to removal from Office, and disqualification to hold and enjoy any Office of honor, Trust or Profit under the United States: but the Party convicted shall nevertheless be liable and subject to Indictment, Trial, Judgment and Punishment, according to Law.

Section. 4   The Times, Places and Manner of holding Elections for Senators and Representatives, shall be prescribed in each State by the Legislature thereof; but the Congress may at any time by Law make or alter such Regulations, except as to the Places of chusing Senators.

The Congress shall assemble at least once in every Year, and such Meeting shall be on the first Monday in December, unless they shall by Law appoint a different Day.

Section. 5   Each House shall be the Judge of the Elections, Returns and Qualifications of its own Members, and a Majority of each shall constitute a Quorum to do Business; but a smaller Number may adjourn from day to day, and may be authorized to compel the Attendance of absent Members, in such Manner, and under such Penalties as each House may provide.

Each House may determine the Rules of its Proceedings, punish its Members for disorderly Behaviour, and, with the Concurrence of two thirds, expel a Member.

Each House shall keep a Journal of its Proceedings, and from time to time publish the same, excepting such Parts as may in their Judgment require Secrecy; and the Yeas and Nays of the Members of either House on any question shall, at the Desire of one fifth of those Present, be entered on the Journal.

Neither House, during the Session of Congress, shall, without the Consent of the other, adjourn for more than three days, nor to any other Place than that in which the two Houses shall be sitting.

Section. 6   The Senators and Representatives shall receive a Compensation for their Services, to be ascertained by Law, and paid out of the Treasury of the United States. They shall in all Cases, except Treason, Felony and Breach of the Peace, be privileged from Arrest during their Attendance at the Session of their respective Houses, and in going to and returning from the same; and for any Speech or Debate in either House, they shall not be questioned in any other Place.

弹劾案的判决，不得超出免职和剥夺担任和享有合众国属下有荣誉、有责任或有薪金的任何职务的资格。但被定罪的人，仍可依法起诉、审判、判决和惩罚。

第四款　举行参议员和众议员选举的时间、地点和方式，在每个州由该州议会规定。但除选举参议员的地点外，国会得随时以法律制定或改变这类规定。

国会每年至少开会一次，除非国会以法律另订日期外，此会议在［十二月第一个星期一］④举行。

第五款　每院是本院议员的选举、选举结果报告和资格的裁判者。每院议员过半数，即构成议事的法定人数；但不足法定人数时，得逐日休会，并有权按每院规定的方式和罚则，强迫缺席议员出席会议。

每院得规定本院议事规则，惩罚本院议员扰乱秩序的行为，并经三之二议员的同意开除议员。

每院应有本院会议记录，并不时予以公布，但它认为需要保密的部分除外。每院议员对于任何问题的赞成票和反对票，在出席议员五分之一的请求下，应载入会议记录。

在国会开会期间，任何一院，未经另一院同意，不得休会三日以上，也不得到非两院开会的任何地方休会。

第六款　参议员和众议员应得到服务的报酬，此项报酬由法律确定并由合众国国库支付。他们除犯叛国罪、重罪和妨害治安罪外，在一切情况下都享有在出席各自议院会议期间和往返于各自议院途中不受逮捕的特权。他们不得因在各自议院发表的演说或辩论而在任何其他地方受到质问。

No Senator or Representative shall, during the Time for which he was elected, be appointed to any civil Office under the Authority of the United States, which shall have been created, or the Emoluments whereof shall have been encreased during such time; and no Person holding any Office under the United States, shall be a Member of either House during his Continuance in Office.

Section. 7   All Bills for raising Revenue shall originate in the House of Representatives; but the Senate may propose or concur with Amendments as on other Bills.

Every Bill which shall have passed the House of Representatives and the Senate, shall, before it become a Law, be presented to the President of the United States: If he approve he shall sign it, but if not he shall return it, with his Objections to that House in which it shall have originated, who shall enter the Objections at large on their Journal, and proceed to reconsider it. If after such Reconsideration two thirds of that House shall agree to pass the Bill, it shall be sent, together with the Objections, to the other House, by which it shall likewise be reconsidered, and if approved by two thirds of that House, it shall become a Law. But in all such Cases the Votes of both Houses shall be determined by yeas and Nays, and the Names of the Persons voting for and against the Bill shall be entered on the Journal of each House respectively. If any Bill shall not be returned by the President within ten Days (Sundays excepted) after it shall have been presented to him, the Same shall be a Law, in like Manner as if he had signed it, unless the Congress by their Adjournment prevent its Return, in which Case it shall not be a Law.

Every Order, Resolution, or Vote to which the Concurrence of the Senate and House of Representatives may be necessary (except on a question of Adjournment) shall be presented to the President of the United States; and before the Same shall take Effect, shall be approved by him, or being disapproved by him, shall be repassed by two thirds of the Senate and House of Representatives, according to the Rules and Limitations prescribed in the Case of a Bill.

Section. 8   The Congress shall have Power To lay and collect Taxes, Duties, Imposts and Excises, to pay the Debts and provide for the common Defence and general Welfare of the United States; but all Duties, Imposts and Excises shall be uniform throughout the United States;

参议员或众议员在当选任期内，不得被任命担任在此期间设置或增薪的合众国管辖下的任何文官职务。凡在合众国属下任职者，在继续任职期间不得担任任何一院议员。

第七款　所有征税议案应首先在众议院提出，但参议院得像对其他议案一样，提出或同意修正案。

众议院和参议院通过的每一议案，在成为法律前须送交合众国总统。总统如批准该议案，即应签署；如不批准，则应将该议案同其反对意见退回最初提出该议案的议院。该院应特此项反对见详细载入本院会议记录并进行复议。如经复议后，该院三分之二议员同意通过该议案，该议案连同反对意见应一起送交另一议院，并同样由该院进行复议，如经该院三分之二议员赞同，该议案即成为法律。但在所有这类情况下，两院表决都由赞成票和反对票决定；对该议案投赞成票和反对票的议员姓名应分别载入每一议院会议记录。如任何议案在送交总统后十天内（星期日除外）未经总统退回，该议案如同总统已签署一样，即成为法律，除非因国会休会而使该议案不能退回，在此种情况下，该议案不能成为法律。

凡须由参议院和众议院一致同意的每项命令、决议或表决（关于休会问题除外），须送交合众国总统，该项命令、决议或表决在生效前，须由总统批准，如总统不批准，则按照关于议案所规定的规则和限制，由参议院和众议院三分之二议员重新通过。

第八款　国会有权：

规定和征收直接税、进口税、捐税和其他税，以偿付国债、提供合众国共同防务和公共福利，但一切进口税、捐税和其他税应全国统一；

To borrow Money on the credit of the United States;

To regulate Commerce with foreign Nations, and among the several States, and with the Indian Tribes;

To establish an uniform Rule of Naturalization, and uniform Laws on the subject of Bankruptcies throughout the United States;

To coin Money, regulate the Value thereof, and of foreign Coin, and fix the Standard of Weights and Measures;

To provide for the Punishment of counterfeiting the Securities and current Coin of the United States;

To establish Post Offices and post Roads;

To promote the Progress of Science and useful Arts, by securing for limited Times to Authors and Inventors the exclusive Right to their respective Writings and Discoveries;

To constitute Tribunals inferior to the supreme Court;

To define and punish Piracies and Felonies committed on the high Seas, and Offences against the Law of Nations;

To declare War, grant Letters of Marque and Reprisal, and make Rules concerning Captures on Land and Water;

To raise and support Armies, but no Appropriation of Money to that Use shall be for a longer Term than two Years;

To provide and maintain a Navy;

To make Rules for the Government and Regulation of the land and naval Forces;

To provide for calling forth the Militia to execute the Laws of the Union, suppress Insurrections and repel Invasions;

To provide for organizing, arming, and disciplining, the Militia, and for governing such Part of them as may be employed in the Service of the United States, reserving to the States respectively, the Appointment of the Officers, and the Authority of training the Militia according to the discipline prescribed by Congress;

以合众国的信用借款；

管制同外国的、各州之间的和同印第安部落的商业；

制定合众国全国统一的归化条例和破产法；

铸造货币，厘定本国货币和外国货币的价值，并确定度量衡的标准；

规定有关伪造合众国证券和通用货币的罚则；

设立邮政局和修建邮政道路；

保障著作家和发明家对各自著作和发明在限定期限内的专有权利，以促进科学和工艺的进步；

设立低于最高法院的法院；

界定和惩罚在公海上所犯的海盗罪和重罪以及违反国际法的犯罪行为；

宣战，颁发掳获敌船许可状，制定关于陆上和水上捕获的条例；

招募陆军和供给军需，但此项用途的拨款期限不得超过两年；

建立和维持一支海军；

制定治理和管理陆海军的条例；

规定征召民兵，以执行联邦法律、镇压叛乱和击退入侵；

规定民兵的组织、装备和训练，规定用来为合众国服役的那些民兵的管理，但民兵军官的任命和按国会规定的条例训练民兵的权力，由各州保留。

To exercise exclusive Legislation in all Cases whatsoever, over such District (not exceeding ten Miles square) as may, by Cession of particular States, and the Acceptance of Congress, become the Seat of the Government of the United States, and to exercise like Authority over all Places purchased by the Consent of the Legislature of the State in which the Same shall be, for the Erection of Forts, Magazines, Arsenals, dock-Yards, and other needful Buildings;--And To make all Laws which shall be necessary and proper for carrying into Execution the foregoing Powers, and all other Powers vested by this Constitution in the Government of the United States, or in any Department or Officer thereof.

Section. 9   The Migration or Importation of such Persons as any of the States now existing shall think proper to admit, shall not be prohibited by the Congress prior to the Year one thousand eight hundred and eight, but a Tax or duty may be imposed on such Importation, not exceeding ten dollars for each Person.

The Privilege of the Writ of Habeas Corpus shall not be suspended, unless when in Cases of Rebellion or Invasion the public Safety may require it.

No Bill of Attainder or ex post facto Law shall be passed.

No Capitation, or other direct, Tax shall be laid, unless in Proportion to the Census or enumeration herein before directed to be taken.

No Tax or Duty shall be laid on Articles exported from any State.

No Preference shall be given by any Regulation of Commerce or Revenue to the Ports of one State over those of another; nor shall Vessels bound to, or from, one State, be obliged to enter, clear, or pay Duties in another.

No Money shall be drawn from the Treasury, but in Consequence of Appropriations made by Law; and a regular Statement and Account of the Receipts and Expenditures of all public Money shall be published from time to time.

No Title of Nobility shall be granted by the United States: And no Person holding any Office of Profit or Trust under them, shall, without the Consent of the Congress, accept of any present, Emolument, Office, or Title, of any kind whatever, from any King, Prince, or foreign State.

对于由某些州让与合众国、经国会接受而成为合众国政府所在地的地区（不得超过十平方英里），在任何情况下都行使独有的立法权；对于经州议会同意、由合众国在该州购买的用于建造要塞、弹药库、兵工厂、船坞和其他必要建筑物的一切地方，行使同样的权力；以及制定为行使上述各项权力和由本宪法授予合众国政府或其任何部门或官员的一切其他权力所必要和适当的所有法律。

第九款　现有任何一州认为得准予入境之人的迁移或入境，在一千八百零八年以前，国会不得加以禁止，但对此种人的入境，每人可征不超过十美元的税。不得中止人身保护状的特权，除非发生叛乱或入侵时公共安全要求中止这项特权。

不得通过公民权利剥夺法案或追溯既往的法律。

［除依本宪法上文规定的人口普查或统计的比例，不得征收人头税或其他直接税。］⑤

对于从任何一州输出的货物，不得征税。

任何商业或税收条例，都不得给予一州港口以优惠于他州港口的待遇；开往或开出一州的船舶，不得被强迫在他州入港、出港或纳税。

除根据法律规定的拨款外，不得从国库提取款项。一切公款收支的定期报告书和账目，应不时予以公布。

合众国不得授予贵族爵位。凡在合众国属下担任任何有薪金或有责任的职务的人，未经国会同意，不得从任何国王、君主或外国接受任何礼物、俸禄、官职或任何一种爵位。

Section. 10   No State shall enter into any Treaty, Alliance, or Confederation; grant Letters of Marque and Reprisal; coin Money; emit Bills of Credit; make any Thing but gold and silver Coin a Tender in Payment of Debts; pass any Bill of Attainder, ex post facto Law, or Law impairing the Obligation of Contracts, or grant any Title of Nobility.

No State shall, without the Consent of the Congress, lay any Imposts or Duties on Imports or Exports, except what may be absolutely necessary for executing it's inspection Laws: and the net Produce of all Duties and Imposts, laid by any State on Imports or Exports, shall be for the Use of the Treasury of the United States; and all such Laws shall be subject to the Revision and Controul of the Congress.

No State shall, without the Consent of Congress, lay any Duty of Tonnage, keep Troops, or Ships of War in time of Peace, enter into any Agreement or Compact with another State, or with a foreign Power, or engage in War, unless actually invaded, or in such imminent Danger as will not admit of delay.

Article. II.

Section. 1   The executive Power shall be vested in a President of the United States of America. He shall hold his Office during the Term of four Years, and, together with the Vice President, chosen for the same Term, be elected, as follows:

Each State shall appoint, in such Manner as the Legislature thereof may direct, a Number of Electors, equal to the whole Number of Senators and Representatives to which the State may be entitled in the Congress: but no Senator or Representative, or Person holding an Office of Trust or Profit under the United States, shall be appointed an Elector.

The Electors shall meet in their respective States, and vote by Ballot for two Persons, of whom one at least shall not be an Inhabitant of the same State with themselves. And they shall make a List of all the Persons voted for, and of the Number of Votes for each; which List they shall sign and certify, and transmit sealed to the Seat of the Government of the United States, directed to the President of the Senate. The President of the Senate shall, in the Presence of the Senate and House of Representatives, open all the Certificates, and the Votes shall then be counted. The Person

第十款　任何一州都不得：缔结任何条约，参加任何同盟或邦联；颁发捕获敌船许可状；铸造货币；发行纸币；使用金银币以外的任何物品作为偿还债务的货币；通过任何公民权利剥夺法案、追溯既往的法律或损害契约义务的法律；或授予任何贵族爵位。

任何一州，未经国会同意，不得对进口货或出口货征收任何税款，但为执行本州检查法所绝对必需者除外。任何一州对进口货或出口货所征全部税款的纯收益供合众国国库使用；所有这类法律得由国会加以修正和控制。

任何一州，未经国会同意，不得征收任何船舶吨位税，不得在和平时期保持军队或战舰，不得与他州或外国缔结协定或盟约，除非实际遭到入侵或遇刻不容缓的紧迫危险时不得进行战争。

第二条

第一款　行政权属于美利坚合众国总统。总统任期四年，副总统的任期相同。总统和副总统按以下方法选举：每个州依照该州议会所定方式选派选举人若干人，其数目同该州在国会应有的参议员和众议员总人数相等。但参议员或众议员，或在合众国属下担任有责任或有薪金职务的人，不得被选派为选举人。

［选举人在各自州内集会，投票选举两人，其中至少有一人不是选举人本州的居民。选举人须开列名单，写明所有被选人和每人所得票数；在该名单上签名作证，将封印后的名单送合众国政府所在地，交参议院议长收。参议院议长在参议院和众议院全体议员面前开拆所有证明书，然后计算票数。得票最多的人，如所得票数超过所选派选举人总数的半数，即为总统。如获得此种过半数票的人不止一人，且得票相等，众议院应立即投票选举其中一人为总统。如无人获得过半数票，该院应以同样方式从名单上得票最多的五人中选举一人为总统。但选举总统时，以州为单位计票，每州代表有一票表决权；三分之二的州各有一名或多名众议员出席，即构成选举总统的法定人数，选出总统需要所有州的过半数票。

having the greatest Number of Votes shall be the President, if such Number be a Majority of the whole Number of Electors appointed; and if there be more than one who have such Majority, and have an equal Number of Votes, then the House of Representatives shall immediately chuse by Ballot one of them for President; and if no Person have a Majority, then from the five highest on the List the said House shall in like Manner chuse the President. But in chusing the President, the Votes shall be taken by States, the Representation from each State having one Vote; A quorum for this purpose shall consist of a Member or Members from two thirds of the States, and a Majority of all the States shall be necessary to a Choice. In every Case, after the Choice of the President, the Person having the greatest Number of Votes of the Electors shall be the Vice President. But if there should remain two or more who have equal Votes, the Senate shall chuse from them by Ballot the Vice President.

The Congress may determine the Time of chusing the Electors, and the Day on which they shall give their Votes; which Day shall be the same throughout the United States.

No Person except a natural born Citizen, or a Citizen of the United States, at the time of the Adoption of this Constitution, shall be eligible to the Office of President; neither shall any Person be eligible to that Office who shall not have attained to the Age of thirty five Years, and been fourteen Years a Resident within the United States.

In Case of the Removal of the President from Office, or of his Death, Resignation, or Inability to discharge the Powers and Duties of the said Office, the Same shall devolve on the Vice President, and the Congress may by Law provide for the Case of Removal, Death, Resignation or Inability, both of the President and Vice President, declaring what Officer shall then act as President, and such Officer shall act accordingly, until the Disability be removed, or a President shall be elected.

The President shall, at stated Times, receive for his Services, a Compensation, which shall neither be increased nor diminished during the Period for which he shall have been elected, and he shall not receive within that Period any other Emolument from the United States, or any of them.

在每种情况下，总统选出后，得选举人票最多的人，即为副总统。但如果有两人或两人以上得票相等，参议院应投票选举其中一人为副总统。]⑥

国会得确定选出选举人的时间和选举人投票日期，该日期在全合众国应为同一天。

无论何人，除生为合众国公民或在本宪法采用时已是合众国公民者外，不得当选为总统；凡年龄不满三十五岁、在合众国境内居住不满十四年者，也不得当选为总统。

[如遇总统被免职、死亡、辞职或丧失履行总统权力和责任的能力时，总统职务应移交副总统。国会得以法律规定在总统和副总统两人被免职、死亡、辞职或丧失任职能力时，宣布应代理总统的官员。该官员应代理总统直到总统恢复任职能力或新总统选出为止。]⑦

总统在规定的时间，应得到服务报酬，此项报酬在其当选担任总统任期内不得增加或减少。总统在任期内不得接受合众国或任何一州的任何其他俸禄。

Before he enter on the Execution of his Office, he shall take the following Oath or Affirmation:--"I do solemnly swear (or affirm) that I will faithfully execute the Office of President of the United States, and will to the best of my Ability, preserve, protect and defend the Constitution of the United States."

Section. 2   The President shall be Commander in Chief of the Army and Navy of the United States, and of the Militia of the several States, when called into the actual Service of the United States; he may require the Opinion, in writing, of the principal Officer in each of the executive Departments, upon any Subject relating to the Duties of their respective Offices, and he shall have Power to grant Reprieves and Pardons for Offences against the United States, except in Cases of Impeachment.

He shall have Power, by and with the Advice and Consent of the Senate, to make Treaties, provided two thirds of the Senators present concur; and he shall nominate, and by and with the Advice and Consent of the Senate, shall appoint Ambassadors, other public Ministers and Consuls, Judges of the supreme Court, and all other Officers of the United States, whose Appointments are not herein otherwise provided for, and which shall be established by Law: but the Congress may by Law vest the Appointment of such inferior Officers, as they think proper, in the President alone, in the Courts of Law, or in the Heads of Departments.

The President shall have Power to fill up all Vacancies that may happen during the Recess of the Senate, by granting Commissions which shall expire at the End of their next Session.

Section. 3   He shall from time to time give to the Congress Information of the State of the Union, and recommend to their Consideration such Measures as he shall judge necessary and expedient; he may, on extraordinary Occasions, convene both Houses, or either of them, and in Case of Disagreement between them, with Respect to the Time of Adjournment, he may adjourn them to such Time as he shall think proper; he shall receive Ambassadors and other public Ministers; he shall take Care that the Laws be faithfully executed, and shall Commission all the Officers of the United States.

Section. 4   The President, Vice President and all civil Officers of the United States, shall be removed from Office on Impeachment for, and Conviction of, Treason, Bribery, or other high Crimes and Misdemeanors.

总统在开始执行职务前，应作如下宣誓或代誓宣言："我庄严宣誓（或宣言）我一定忠实执行合众国总统职务，竭尽全力维护、保护和捍卫合众国宪法"。

第二款　总统是合众国陆军、海军和征调为合众国服役的各州民兵的总司令。他得要求每个行政部门长官就他们各自职责有关的任何事项提出书面意见。他有权对危害合众国的犯罪行为发布缓刑令和赦免令，但弹劾案除外。

总统经咨询参议院和取得其同意有权缔结条约，但须经出席参议员三分之二的批准。他提名，并经咨询参议院和取得其同意，任命大使、公使和领事、最高法院法官和任命手续未由本宪法另行规定而应由法律规定的合众国所有其他官员。但国会认为适当时，得以法律将这类低级官员的任命权授予总统一人、法院或各部部长。

总统有权委任人员填补在参议院休会期间可能出现的官员缺额，此项委任在参议院下期会议结束时满期。

第三款　总统应不时向国会报告联邦情况，并向国会提出他认为必要和妥善的措施供国会审议。在非常情况下，他得召集两院或任何一院开会。如遇两院对休会时间有意见分歧时，他可使两院休会到他认为适当的时间。他应接见大使和公使。他应负责使法律切实执行，并委任合众国的所有官员。

第四款　总统、副总统和合众国的所有文职官员，因叛国、贿赂或其他重罪和轻罪而受弹劾并被定罪时，应予免职。

Article III.

Section. 1   The judicial Power of the United States shall be vested in one supreme Court, and in such inferior Courts as the Congress may from time to time ordain and establish. The Judges, both of the supreme and inferior Courts, shall hold their Offices during good Behaviour, and shall, at stated Times, receive for their Services a Compensation, which shall not be diminished during their Continuance in Office.

Section. 2   The judicial Power shall extend to all Cases, in Law and Equity, arising under this Constitution, the Laws of the United States, and Treaties made, or which shall be made, under their Authority;--to all Cases affecting Ambassadors, other public Ministers and Consuls;--to all Cases of admiralty and maritime Jurisdiction;--to Controversies to which the United States shall be a Party;--to Controversies between two or more States;-- between a State and Citizens of another State,--between Citizens of different States,--between Citizens of the same State claiming Lands under Grants of different States, and between a State, or the Citizens thereof, and foreign States, Citizens or Subjects.

In all Cases affecting Ambassadors, other public Ministers and Consuls, and those in which a State shall be Party, the supreme Court shall have original Jurisdiction. In all the other Cases before mentioned, the supreme Court shall have appellate Jurisdiction, both as to Law and Fact, with such Exceptions, and under such Regulations as the Congress shall make.

The Trial of all Crimes, except in Cases of Impeachment, shall be by Jury; and such Trial shall be held in the State where the said Crimes shall have been committed; but when not committed within any State, the Trial shall be at such Place or Places as the Congress may by Law have directed.

Section. 3   Treason against the United States, shall consist only in levying War against them, or in adhering to their Enemies, giving them Aid and Comfort. No Person shall be convicted of Treason unless on the Testimony of two Witnesses to the same overt Act, or on Confession in open Court.

The Congress shall have Power to declare the Punishment of Treason, but no Attainder of Treason shall work Corruption of Blood, or Forfeiture except during the Life of the Person attainted.

第三条

第一款　合众国的司法权，属于最高法院和国会不时规定和设立的下级法院。最高法院和下级法院的法官如行为端正，得继续任职，并应在规定的时间得到服务报酬，此项报酬在他们继续任职期间不得减少。

第二款　司法权的适用范围包括：由于本宪法、合众国法律和根据合众国权力已缔结或将缔结的条约而产生的一切普通法的和衡平法的案件；涉及大使、公使和领事的一切案件；关于海事法和海事管辖权的一切案件；合众国为一方当事人的诉讼；两个或两个以上州之间的诉讼；〔一州和他州公民之间的诉讼；〕⑧不同州公民之间的诉讼；同州公民之间对不同州让与土地的所有权的诉讼；一州或其公民同外国或外国公民或国民之间的诉讼。

涉及大使、公使和领事以及一州为一方当事人的一切案件，最高法院具有第一审管辖权。对上述所有其他案件，不论法律方面还是事实方面，最高法院具有上诉审管辖权，但须依照国会所规定的例外和规章。

除弹劾案外，一切犯罪由陪审团审判；此种审判应在犯罪发生的州内举行；但如犯罪不发生在任何一州之内，审判应在国会以法律规定的一个或几个地点举行。

第三款　对合众国的叛国罪只限于同合众国作战，或依附其敌人，给予其敌人以帮助和鼓励。无论何人，除根据两个证人对同一明显行为的作证或本人在公开法庭上的供认，不得被定为叛国罪。

国会有权宣告对叛国罪的惩罚，但因叛国罪而剥夺公民权，不得造成血统玷污，除非在被剥夺者在世期间，也不得没收其财产。

Article. IV.

Section. 1   Full Faith and Credit shall be given in each State to the public Acts, Records, and judicial Proceedings of every other State. And the Congress may by general Laws prescribe the Manner in which such Acts, Records and Proceedings shall be proved, and the Effect thereof.

Section. 2   The Citizens of each State shall be entitled to all Privileges and Immunities of Citizens in the several States.

A Person charged in any State with Treason, Felony, or other Crime, who shall flee from Justice, and be found in another State, shall on Demand of the executive Authority of the State from which he fled, be delivered up, to be removed to the State having Jurisdiction of the Crime.

No Person held to Service or Labour in one State, under the Laws thereof, escaping into another, shall, in Consequence of any Law or Regulation therein, be discharged from such Service or Labour, but shall be delivered up on Claim of the Party to whom such Service or Labour may be due.

Section. 3   New States may be admitted by the Congress into this Union; but no new State shall be formed or erected within the Jurisdiction of any other State; nor any State be formed by the Junction of two or more States, or Parts of States, without the Consent of the Legislatures of the States concerned as well as of the Congress.

The Congress shall have Power to dispose of and make all needful Rules and Regulations respecting the Territory or other Property belonging to the United States; and nothing in this Constitution shall be so construed as to Prejudice any Claims of the United States, or of any particular State.

Section. 4   The United States shall guarantee to every State in this Union a Republican Form of Government, and shall protect each of them against Invasion; and on Application of the Legislature, or of the Executive (when the Legislature cannot be convened), against domestic Violence.

第四条

第一款　每个州对于他州的公共法律、案卷和司法程序，应给予充分信任和尊重。国会得以一般法律规定这类法律、案卷和司法程序如何证明和具有的效力。

第二款　每个州的公民享有各州公民的一切特权和豁免权。

在任何一州被控告犯有叛国罪、重罪或其他罪行的人，逃脱法网而在他州被寻获时，应根据他所逃出之州行政当局的要求将他交出，以便解送到对犯罪行为有管辖权的州。

［根据一州法律须在该州服劳役或劳动的人，如逃往他州，不得因他州的法律或规章而免除此种劳役或劳动，而应根据有权得到此劳役或劳动之当事人的要求将他交出。］⑨

第三款　新州得由国会接纳加入本联邦；但不得在任何其他州的管辖范围内组成或建立新州；未经有关州议会和国会的同意，也不得合并两个或两个以上的州或几个州的一部分组成新州。

国会对于属于合众国的领土或其他财产，有权处置和制定一切必要的条例和规章。对本宪法条文不得作有损于合众国或任何一州的任何权利的解释。

第四款　合众国保证本联邦各州实行共和政体，保护每州免遭入侵，并应州议会或州行政长官（在州议会不能召开时）的请求平定内乱。

Article. V.

The·Congress, whenever two thirds of both Houses shall deem it necessary, shall propose Amendments to this Constitution, or, on the Application of the Legislatures of two thirds of the several States, shall call a Convention for proposing Amendments, which, in either Case, shall be valid to all Intents and Purposes, as Part of this Constitution, when ratified by the Legislatures of three fourths of the several States, or by Conventions in three fourths thereof, as the one or the other Mode of Ratification may be proposed by the Congress; Provided that no Amendment which may be made prior to the Year One thousand eight hundred and eight shall in any Manner affect the first and fourth Clauses in the Ninth Section of the first Article; and that no State, without its Consent, shall be deprived of its equal Suffrage in the Senate.

Article. VI.

All Debts contracted and Engagements entered into, before the Adoption of this Constitution, shall be as valid against the United States under this Constitution, as under the Confederation.

This Constitution, and the Laws of the United States which shall be made in Pursuance thereof; and all Treaties made, or which shall be made, under the Authority of the United States, shall be the supreme Law of the Land; and the Judges in every State shall be bound thereby, any Thing in the Constitution or Laws of any State to the Contrary notwithstanding.

The Senators and Representatives before mentioned, and the Members of the several State Legislatures, and all executive and judicial Officers, both of the United States and of the several States, shall be bound by Oath or Affirmation, to support this Constitution; but no religious Test shall ever be required as a Qualification to any Office or public Trust under the United States.

Article. VII.

The Ratification of the Conventions of nine States, shall be sufficient for the Establishment of this Constitution between the States so ratifying the Same.

第五条

国会在两院三分之二议员认为必要时，应提出本宪法的修正案，或根据各州三分之二州议会的请求，召开制宪会议提出修正案。不论哪种方式提出的修正案，经各州四分之三州议会或四分之三州制宪会议的批准，即实际成为本宪法的一部分而发生效力；采用哪种批准方式，得由国会提出建议。但［在一千八百零八年以前制定的修正案，不得以任何形式影响本宪法第一条第九款第一项和第四项］；⑩任何一州，不经其同意，不得被剥夺它在参议院的平等投票权。

第六条

本宪法采用前订立的一切债务和承担的一切义务，对于实行本宪法的合众国同邦联时期一样有效。

本宪法和依本宪法所制定的合众国法律，以及根据合众国的权力已缔结或将缔结的一切条约，都是全国的最高法律；每个州的法官都应受其约束，即使州的宪法和法律中有与之相抵触的内容。

上述参议员和众议员，各州州议会议员，以及合众国和各州所有行政和司法官员，应宣誓或作代誓宣言拥护本宪法；但决不得以宗教信仰作为担任合众国属下任何官职或公职的必要资格。

第七条

经九个州制宪会议的批准，即足以使本宪法在各批准州成立。

Done in Convention by the Unanimous Consent of the States present the Seventeenth Day of September in the Year of our Lord one thousand seven hundred and Eighty seven and of the Independance of the United States of America the Twelfth In witness whereof We have hereunto subscribed our Names.

G°. Washington

Presidt and deputy from Virginia

Delaware

Geo: Read   Gunning Bedford jun

John Dickinson   Richard Bassett

Jaco: Broom

Maryland

James McHenry   Dan of St Thos. Jenifer

Danl. Carroll

Virginia

John Blair   James Madison Jr.

North Carolina

Wm. Blount   Richd. Dobbs Spaight

Hu Williamson

South Carolina

J. Rutledge   Charles Cotesworth Pinckney

Charles Pinckney   Pierce Butler

Georgia

William Few   Abr Baldwin

New Hampshire

John Langdon   Nicholas Gilman

本宪法于耶稣纪元一千七百八十七年，即美利坚合众国独立后第十二年的九月十七日，经出席各州在制宪会议上一致同意后制定。我们谨在此签名作证。

乔治·华盛顿
主席、弗吉尼亚州代表
特拉华州

　　乔治·里德　　　　　　　　小冈宁·贝德福德

　　约翰·迪金森　　　　　　　理查德·巴西特

　　雅各布·布鲁姆

马里兰州

　　詹姆斯·麦克亨利　　　　　圣托马斯·詹尼弗的丹尼尔

　　丹尼尔·卡罗尔

弗吉尼亚州

　　约翰·布莱尔　　　　　　　小詹姆斯·麦迪逊

北卡罗来纳州

　　威廉·布朗特　　　　　　　理查德·多布斯·斯佩特

　　休·威廉森

南卡罗来纳州

　　约翰·拉特利奇　　　　　　查尔斯·科茨沃斯·平克尼

　　查尔斯·平克尼　　　　　　皮尔斯·巴特勒

佐治亚州

　　威廉·费尤　　　　　　　　亚伯拉罕·鲍德温

新罕布什尔州

　　约翰·兰登　　　　　　　　尼古拉斯·吉尔曼

Massachusetts

| Nathaniel Gorham | Rufus King |

Connecticut

| Wm. Saml. Johnson | Roger Sherman |

New York

Alexander Hamilton

New Jersey

| Wil: Livingston | David Brearley |
| Wm. Paterson | Jona: Dayton |

Pennsylvania

B Franklin	Thomas Mifflin
Robt. Morris	Geo. Clymer
Thos. FitzSimons	Jared Ingersoll
James Wilson	Gouv Morris

Attest William Jackson Secretary

The Bill of Rights:

Amendment I

Congress shall make no law respecting an establishment of religion, or prohibiting the free exercise thereof; or abridging the freedom of speech, or of the press; or the right of the people peaceably to assemble, and to petition the Government for a redress of grievances.

马萨诸塞州

　　纳撒尼尔·戈勒姆　　　　　　鲁弗斯·金

康涅狄格州

　　威廉·塞缪尔·约翰逊　　　　罗杰·谢尔曼

纽约州

　　亚历山大·汉密尔顿

新泽西州

　　威廉·利文斯顿　　　　　　　戴维·布里尔利

　　威廉·帕特森　　　　　　　　乔纳森·戴顿

宾夕法尼亚州

　　本杰明·富兰克林　　　　　　托马斯·米夫林

　　罗伯特·莫里斯　　　　　　　乔治·克莱默

　　托马斯·菲茨西蒙斯　　　　　贾雷德·英格索尔

　　詹姆斯·威尔逊　　　　　　　古·莫里斯

　　证人：威廉·杰克逊，秘书

《权利法案》：

　　（依照原宪法第五条、由国会提出并经各州批准、增添和修改美利坚合众国宪法的条款。译者注）

第一条修正案

　　［前十条修正案于 1789 年 9 月 25 日提出，1791 年 12 月 15 日批准，被称为"权利法案"。］

　　国会不得制定关于下列事项的法律：确立国教或禁止信教自由；剥夺言论自由或出版自由；或剥夺人民和平集会和向政府请愿伸冤的权利。

Amendment II

A well regulated Militia, being necessary to the security of a free State, the right of the people to keep and bear Arms, shall not be infringed.

Amendment III

No Soldier shall, in time of peace be quartered in any house, without the consent of the Owner, nor in time of war, but in a manner to be prescribed by law.

Amendment IV

The right of the people to be secure in their persons, houses, papers, and effects, against unreasonable searches and seizures, shall not be violated, and no Warrants shall issue, but upon probable cause, supported by Oath or affirmation, and particularly describing the place to be searched, and the persons or things to be seized.

Amendment V

No person shall be held to answer for a capital, or otherwise infamous crime, unless on a presentment or indictment of a Grand Jury, except in cases arising in the land or naval forces, or in the Militia, when in actual service in time of War or public danger; nor shall any person be subject for the same offence to be twice put in jeopardy of life or limb; nor shall be compelled in any criminal case to be a witness against himself, nor be deprived of life, liberty, or property, without due process of law; nor shall private property be taken for public use, without just compensation.

Amendment VI

In all criminal prosecutions, the accused shall enjoy the right to a speedy and public trial, by an impartial jury of the State and district wherein the crime shall have been committed, which district shall have been previously ascertained by law, and to be informed of the nature and cause of the accusation; to be confronted with the witnesses against him; to have compulsory process for obtaining witnesses in his favor, and to have the Assistance of Counsel for his defence.

第二条修正案

管理良好的民兵是保障自由州的安全所必需的，因此人民持有和携带武器的权利不得侵犯。

第三条修正案

未经房主同意，士兵平时不得驻扎在任何住宅；除依法律规定的方式，战时也不得驻扎。

第四条修正案

人民的人身、住宅、文件和财产不受无理搜查和扣押的权利，不得侵犯。除依据可能成立的理由，以宣誓或代誓宣言保证，并详细说明搜查地点和扣押的人或物，不得发出搜查和扣押状。

第五条修正案

无论何人，除非根据大陪审团的报告或起诉书，不受死罪或其他重罪的审判，但发生在陆、海军中或发生在战时或出现公共危险时服役的民兵中的案件除外。任何人不得因同一犯罪行为而两次遭受生命或身体的危害；不得在任何刑事案件中被迫自证其罪；不经正当法律程序，不得被剥夺生命、自由或财产。不给予公平赔偿，私有财产不得充作公用。

第六条修正案

在一切刑事诉讼中，被告有权由犯罪行为发生地的州和地区的公正陪审团予以迅速和公开的审判，该地区应事先已由法律确定；得知控告的性质和理由；同原告证人对质；以强制程序取得对其有利的证人；取得律师帮助为其辩护。

Amendment VII

In Suits at common law, where the value in controversy shall exceed twenty dollars, the right of trial by jury shall be preserved, and no fact tried by a jury, shall be otherwise re-examined in any Court of the United States, than according to the rules of the common law.

Amendment VIII

Excessive bail shall not be required, nor excessive fines imposed, nor cruel and unusual punishments inflicted.

Amendment IX

The enumeration in the Constitution, of certain rights, shall not be construed to deny or disparage others retained by the people.

Amendment X

The powers not delegated to the United States by the Constitution, nor prohibited by it to the States, are reserved to the States respectively, or to the people.

The Constitution: Amendments 11-27

AMENDMENT XI

Passed by Congress March 4, 1794. Ratified February 7, 1795.

Note: Article III, section 2, of the Constitution was modified by amendment 11.

The Judicial power of the United States shall not be construed to extend to any suit in law or equity, commenced or prosecuted against one of the United States by Citizens of another State, or by Citizens or Subjects of any Foreign State.

第七条修正案

在习惯法的诉讼中，其争执价额超过二十美元，由陪审团审判的权利应受到保护。由陪审团裁决的事实，合众国的任何法院除非按照习惯法规则，不得重新审查。

第八条修正案

不得要求过多的保释金，不得处以过重的罚金，不得施加残酷和非常的惩罚。

第九条修正案

本宪法对某些权利的列举，不得被解释为否定或轻视由人民保留的其他权利。

第十条修正案

宪法未授予合众国、也未禁止各州行使的权力，由各州各自保留，或由人民保留。

第十一条修正案

［1794 年 3 月 4 日提出，1795 年 2 月 7 日批准］

合众国的司法权，不得被解释为适用于由他州公民或任何外国公民或国民对合众国一州提出的或起诉的任何普通法或衡平法的诉讼。

AMENDMENT XII

Passed by Congress December 9, 1803. Ratified June 15, 1804.

Note: A portion of Article II, section 1 of the Constitution was superseded by the 12th amendment.

The Electors shall meet in their respective states and vote by ballot for President and Vice-President, one of whom, at least, shall not be an inhabitant of the same state with themselves; they shall name in their ballots the person voted for as President, and in distinct ballots the person voted for as Vice-President, and they shall make distinct lists of all persons voted for as President, and of all persons voted for as Vice-President, and of the number of votes for each, which lists they shall sign and certify, and transmit sealed to the seat of the government of the United States, directed to the President of the Senate; -- the President of the Senate shall, in the presence of the Senate and House of Representatives, open all the certificates and the votes shall then be counted; -- The person having the greatest number of votes for President, shall be the President, if such number be a majority of the whole number of Electors appointed; and if no person have such majority, then from the persons having the highest numbers not exceeding three on the list of those voted for as President, the House of Representatives shall choose immediately, by ballot, the President. But in choosing the President, the votes shall be taken by states, the representation from each state having one vote; a quorum for this purpose shall consist of a member or members from two-thirds of the states, and a majority of all the states shall be necessary to a choice. [And if the House of Representatives shall not choose a President whenever the right of choice shall devolve upon them, before the fourth day of March next following, then the Vice-President shall act as President, as in case of the death or other constitutional disability of the President. --]* The person having the greatest number of votes as Vice-President, shall be the Vice-President, if such number be a majority of the whole number of Electors appointed, and if no person have a majority, then from the two highest numbers on the list, the Senate shall choose the Vice-President; a quorum for the purpose shall consist of two-thirds of the whole number of Senators, and a majority of the whole number shall be necessary to a choice. But no person constitutionally ineligible to the office of President shall be eligible to that of Vice-President of the United States.

第十二条修正案

［1803 年 12 月 9 日提出，1804 年 7 月 27 日批准］

选举人在各自州内集会，投票选举总统和副总统，其中至少有一人不是选举人本州的居民。选举人须在选票上写明被选为总统之人的姓名，并在另一选票上写明校选为副总统之人的姓名。选举人须将所有被选为总统之人和所有被选为副总统之人分别开列名单，写明每人所得票数；在该名单上签名作证，将封印后的名单送合众国政府所在地，交参议院议长收。参议院议长在参议院和众议院全体议员面前开拆所有证明书，然后计算票数。获得总统选票最多的人，如所得票数超过所选派选举人总数的半数，即为总统。如无人获得这种过半数票，众议院应立即从被选为总统之人名单中得票最多的但不超过三人中间，投票选举总统。但选举总统时，以州为单位计票，每州代表有一票表决权。三分之二的州各有一名或多名众议员出席，即构成选举总统的法定人数，选出总统需要所有州的过半数票。［当选举总统的权力转移到众议院时，如该院在次年三月四日前尚未选出总统，则由副总统代理总统，如同总统死亡或宪法规定的其他丧失任职能力的情况一样。］(11)得副总统选票最多的人，如所得票数超过所选派选举人总数的半数，即为副总统。如无人得过半数票，参议院应从名单上得票最多的两人中选举副总统。选举副总统的法定人数由参议员总数的三分之二构成，选出副总统需要参议员总数的过半数票。但依宪法无资格担任总统的人，也无资格担任合众国副总统。

*Superseded by section 3 of the 20th amendment.

AMENDMENT XIII

Passed by Congress January 31, 1865. Ratified December 6, 1865.

Note: A portion of Article IV, section 2, of the Constitution was superseded by the 13th amendment.

Section 1   Neither slavery nor involuntary servitude, except as a punishment for crime whereof the party shall have been duly convicted, shall exist within the United States, or any place subject to their jurisdiction.

Section 2   Congress shall have power to enforce this article by appropriate legislation.

AMENDMENT XIV

Passed by Congress June 13, 1866. Ratified July 9, 1868.

Note: Article I, section 2, of the Constitution was modified by section 2 of the 14th amendment.

Section 1   All persons born or naturalized in the United States, and subject to the jurisdiction thereof, are citizens of the United States and of the State wherein they reside. No State shall make or enforce any law which shall abridge the privileges or immunities of citizens of the United States; nor shall any State deprive any person of life, liberty, or property, without due process of law; nor deny to any person within its jurisdiction the equal protection of the laws.

Section 2   Representatives shall be apportioned among the several States according to their respective numbers, counting the whole number of persons in each State, excluding Indians not taxed. But when the right to vote at any election for the choice of electors for President and Vice-President of the United States, Representatives in Congress, the Executive and Judicial officers of a State, or the members of the Legislature thereof, is denied to any of the male inhabitants of such State, being twenty-one years of age,* and citizens of the United States, or in any way abridged, except for participation in rebellion, or other crime, the basis of representation therein shall be reduced in the proportion which the number of such male citizens shall bear to the whole number of male citizens twenty-one years of age in such State.

第十三条修正案

［1865 年 1 月 31 日提出，1865 年 12 月 6 日批准］

第一款　在合众国境内受合众国管辖的任何地方，奴隶制和强制劳役都不得存在，但作为对于依法判罪的人的犯罪的惩罚除

第二款　国会有权以适当立法实施本条。

第十四条修正案

［1866 年 6 月 13 日提出，1868 年 7 月 9 日批准］

第一款　所有在合众国出生或归化合众国并受其管辖的人，都是合众国的和他们居住州的公民。任何一州，都不得制定或实施限制合众国公民的特权或豁免权的任何法律；不经正当法律程序，不得剥夺任何人的生命、自由或财产；在州管辖范围内，也不得拒绝给予任何人以平等法律保护。

第二款　众议员名额，应按各州人口比例进行分配，此人口数包括一州的全部人口数，但不包括未被征税的印第安人。但在选举合众国总统和副总统选举人、国会众议员、州行政和司法官员或州议会议员的任何选举中，一州的［年满二十一岁］⑰ 并且是合众国公民的任何男性居民，除因参加叛乱或其他犯罪外，如其选举权道到拒绝或受到任何方式的限制，则该州代表权的基础，应按以上男性公民的人数同该州年满二十一岁男性公民总人数的比例予以削减。

Section 3   No person shall be a Senator or Representative in Congress, or elector of President and Vice-President, or hold any office, civil or military, under the United States, or under any State, who, having previously taken an oath, as a member of Congress, or as an officer of the United States, or as a member of any State legislature, or as an executive or judicial officer of any State, to support the Constitution of the United States, shall have engaged in insurrection or rebellion against the same, or given aid or comfort to the enemies thereof. But Congress may by a vote of two-thirds of each House, remove such disability.

Section 4   The validity of the public debt of the United States, authorized by law, including debts incurred for payment of pensions and bounties for services in suppressing insurrection or rebellion, shall not be questioned. But neither the United States nor any State shall assume or pay any debt or obligation incurred in aid of insurrection or rebellion against the United States, or any claim for the loss or emancipation of any slave; but all such debts, obligations and claims shall be held illegal and void.

Section 5   The Congress shall have the power to enforce, by appropriate legislation, the provisions of this article.

*Changed by section 1 of the 26th amendment.

AMENDMENT XV

Passed by Congress February 26, 1869. Ratified February 3, 1870.

Section 1   The right of citizens of the United States to vote shall not be denied or abridged by the United States or by any State on account of race, color, or previous condition of servitude--

Section 2   The Congress shall have the power to enforce this article by appropriate legislation.

AMENDMENT XVI

Passed by Congress July 2, 1909. Ratified February 3, 1913.

Note: Article I, section 9, of the Constitution was modified by amendment 16.

第三款　无论何人，凡先前曾以国会议员、或合众国官员、或任何州议会议员、或任何州行政或司法官员的身份宣誓维护合众国宪法，以后又对合众国作乱或反叛，或给予合众国敌人帮助或鼓励，都不得担任国会参议员或众议员、或总统和副总统选举人，或担任合众国或任何州属下的任何文职或军职官员。但国会得以两院各三分之二的票数取消此种限制。

第四款　对于法律批准的合众国公共债务，包括因支付平定作乱或反叛有功人员的年金和奖金而产生的债务，其效力不得有所怀疑。但无论合众国或任何一州，都不得承担或偿付因援助对合众国的作乱或反叛而产生的任何债务或义务，或因丧失或解放任何奴隶而提出的任何赔偿要求；所有这类债务、义务和要求，都应被认为是非法和无效的。

第五款　国会有权以适当立法实施本条规定。

第十五条修正案
［1869 年 2 月 26 日提出，1870 年 2 月 3 日批准］

第一款　合众国公民的选举权，不得因种族、肤色或以前是奴隶而被合众国或任何一州加以拒绝或限制。

第二款　国会有权以适当立法实施本条。

第十六条修正案
［1909 年 7 月 12 日提出，1913 年 2 月 3 日批准］

The Congress shall have power to lay and collect taxes on incomes, from whatever source derived, without apportionment among the several States, and without regard to any census or enumeration.

AMENDMENT XVII

Passed by Congress May 13, 1912. Ratified April 8, 1913.

Note: Article I, section 3, of the Constitution was modified by the 17th amendment.

The Senate of the United States shall be composed of two Senators from each State, elected by the people thereof, for six years; and each Senator shall have one vote. The electors in each State shall have the qualifications requisite for electors of the most numerous branch of the State legislatures.

When vacancies happen in the representation of any State in the Senate, the executive authority of such State shall issue writs of election to fill such vacancies: Provided, That the legislature of any State may empower the executive thereof to make temporary appointments until the people fill the vacancies by election as the legislature may direct.

This amendment shall not be so construed as to affect the election or term of any Senator chosen before it becomes valid as part of the Constitution.

AMENDMENT XVIII

Passed by Congress December 18, 1917. Ratified January 16, 1919. Repealed by amendment 21.

Section 1   After one year from the ratification of this article the manufacture, sale, or transportation of intoxicating liquors within, the importation thereof into, or the exportation thereof from the United States and all territory subject to the jurisdiction thereof for beverage purposes is hereby prohibited.

Section 2   The Congress and the several States shall have concurrent power to enforce this article by appropriate legislation.

Section 3   This article shall be inoperative unless it shall have been ratified as an amendment to the Constitution by the legislatures of the several States, as provided in the Constitution, within seven years from the date of the submission hereof to the States by the Congress.

　　国会有权对任何来源的收入规定和征收所得税，无须在各州按比例进行分配，也无须考虑任何人口普查或人口统计。

第十七条修正案

〔1912 年 5 月 13 日提出，1913 年 4 月 8 日批准〕

　　合众国参议院由每州人民选举的两名参议员组成，任期六年；每名参议员有一票表决权。每个州的选举人应具备该州州议会人数最多一院选举人所必需的资格。

　　任何一州在参议院的代表出现缺额时，该州行政当局应发布选举令，以填补此项缺额。但任何一州的议会，在人民依该议会指示举行选举填补缺额以前，得授权本州行政长官任命临时参议员。

　　本条修正案不得作如此解释，以致影响在本条修正案作为宪法的一部分生效以前当选的任何参议员的选举或任期。

第十八条修正案

〔1917 年 12 月 18 日提出，1919 年 1 月 16 日批准〕

　　〔第一款　本条批准一年后，禁止在合众国及其管辖下的一切领土内酿造、出售和运送作为饮料的致醉酒类；禁止此类酒类输入或输出合众国及其管辖下的一切领土。

　　第二款　国会和各州都有权以适当立法实施本条。

　　第三款　本条除非在国会将其提交各州之日起七年以内，由各州议会按本宪法规定批准为宪法修正案，不得发生效力。〕⑬

AMENDMENT XIX

Passed by Congress June 4, 1919. Ratified August 18, 1920.

The right of citizens of the United States to vote shall not be denied or abridged by the United States or by any State on account of sex.

Congress shall have power to enforce this article by appropriate legislation.

AMENDMENT XX

Passed by Congress March 2, 1932. Ratified January 23, 1933.

Note: Article I, section 4, of the Constitution was modified by section 2 of this amendment. In addition, a portion of the 12th amendment was superseded by section 3.

Section 1   The terms of the President and the Vice President shall end at noon on the 20th day of January, and the terms of Senators and Representatives at noon on the 3d day of January, of the years in which such terms would have ended if this article had not been ratified; and the terms of their successors shall then begin.

Section 2   The Congress shall assemble at least once in every year, and such meeting shall begin at noon on the 3d day of January, unless they shall by law appoint a different day.

Section 3   If, at the time fixed for the beginning of the term of the President, the President elect shall have died, the Vice President elect shall become President. If a President shall not have been chosen before the time fixed for the beginning of his term, or if the President elect shall have failed to qualify, then the Vice President elect shall act as President until a President shall have qualified; and the Congress may by law provide for the case wherein neither a President elect nor a Vice President shall have qualified, declaring who shall then act as President, or the manner in which one who is to act shall be selected, and such person shall act accordingly until a President or Vice President shall have qualified.

第十九条修正案

［1919 年 6 月 4 日提出，1920 年 8 月 18 日批准］

合众国公民的选举权，不得因性别而被合众国或任何一州加以拒绝或限制。

国会有权以适当立法实施本条。

第二十条修正案

［1933 年 3 月 2 日提出，1933 年 1 月 23 日批准］

第一款　总统和副总统的任期应在本条未获批准前原定任期届满之年的一月二十日正午结束，参议员和众议员的任期在本条未获批准前原定任期届满之年的一月三日正午结束，他们继任人的任期在同时开始。

第二款　国会每年至少应开会一次，除国会以法律另订日期外，此会议在一月三日正午开始。

第三款　如当选总统在规定总统任期开始的时间已经死亡，当选副总统应成为总统。如在规定总统任期开始的时间以前，总统尚未选出，或当选总统不合乎资格，则当选副总统应代理总统直到一名总统已合乎资格时为止。在当选总统和当选副总统都不合乎资格时，国会得以法律规定代理总统之人，或宣布选出代理总统的办法。此人应代理总统直到一名总统或副总统合乎资格时为止。

Section 4 The Congress may by law provide for the case of the death of any of the persons from whom the House of Representatives may choose a President whenever the right of choice shall have devolved upon them, and for the case of the death of any of the persons from whom the Senate may choose a Vice President whenever the right of choice shall have devolved upon them.

Section 5 Sections 1 and 2 shall take effect on the 15th day of October following the ratification of this article.

Section 6 This article shall be inoperative unless it shall have been ratified as an amendment to the Constitution by the legislatures of three-fourths of the several States within seven years from the date of its submission.

AMENDMENT XXI

Passed by Congress February 20, 1933. Ratified December 5, 1933.

Section 1 The eighteenth article of amendment to the Constitution of the United States is hereby repealed.

Section 2 The transportation or importation into any State, Territory, or Possession of the United States for delivery or use therein of intoxicating liquors, in violation of the laws thereof, is hereby prohibited.

Section 3 This article shall be inoperative unless it shall have been ratified as an amendment to the Constitution by conventions in the several States, as provided in the Constitution, within seven years from the date of the submission hereof to the States by the Congress.

AMENDMENT XXII

Passed by Congress March 21, 1947. Ratified February 27, 1951.

Section 1 No person shall be elected to the office of the President more than twice, and no person who has held the office of President, or acted as President, for more than two years of a term to which some other person was elected President shall be elected to the office of President more than once. But this Article shall not apply to any person holding the office of President when this Article was proposed by Congress, and shall not prevent any person who may be holding the office of President, or acting as President, during the term within which this Article becomes operative from holding the office of President or acting as President during the remainder of such term.

第四款　国会得以法律对以下情况作出规定：在选举总统的权利转移到众议院时，而可被该院选为总统的人中有人死亡；在选举副总统的权利转移到参议院时，而可被该院选为副总统的人中有人死亡。

第五款　第一款和第二款应在本条批准以后的十月十五日生效。

第六款　本条除非在其提交各州之日起七年以内，自四分之三州议会批准为宪法修正案，不得发生效力。

第二十一条修正案

[1933 年 2 月 20 日提出，1933 年 12 月 5 日批准]

第一款　美利坚合众国宪法修正案第十八条现予废除。

第二款　在合众国任何州、领地或属地内，凡违反当地法律为在当地发货或使用而运送或输入致醉酒类，均予以禁止。

第三款　本条除非在国会将其提交各州之日起七年以内，由各州制宪会议依本宪法规定批准为宪法修正案，不得发生效力。

第二十二条修正案

[1947 年 3 月 24 日提出，1951 年 2 月 27 日批准]

第一款　无论何人，当选担任总统职务不得超过两次；无论何人，在他人当选总统任期内担任总统职务或代理总统两年以上，不得当选担任总统职务一次以上。但本条不适用于在国会提出本条时正在担任总统职务的任何人；也不妨碍本条在一届总统任期内生效时正在担任总统职务或代理总统的任何人，在此届任期结束前继续担任总统职务或代理总统。

Section 2   This article shall be inoperative unless it shall have been ratified as an amendment to the Constitution by the legislatures of three-fourths of the several States within seven years from the date of its submission to the States by the Congress.

AMENDMENT XXIII

Passed by Congress June 16, 1960. Ratified March 29, 1961.

Section 1   The District constituting the seat of Government of the United States shall appoint in such manner as Congress may direct:

A number of electors of President and Vice President equal to the whole number of Senators and Representatives in Congress to which the District would be entitled if it were a State, but in no event more than the least populous State; they shall be in addition to those appointed by the States, but they shall be considered, for the purposes of the election of President and Vice President, to be electors appointed by a State; and they shall meet in the District and perform such duties as provided by the twelfth article of amendment.

Section 2   The Congress shall have power to enforce this article by appropriate legislation.

AMENDMENT XXIV

Passed by Congress August 27, 1962. Ratified January 23, 1964.

Section 1   The right of citizens of the United States to vote in any primary or other election for President or Vice President, for electors for President or Vice President, or for Senator or Representative in Congress, shall not be denied or abridged by the United States or any State by reason of failure to pay poll tax or other tax.

Section 2   The Congress shall have power to enforce this article by appropriate legislation.

AMENDMENT XXV

Passed by Congress July 6, 1965. Ratified February 10, 1967.

Note: Article II, section 1, of the Constitution was affected by the 25th amendment.

第二款　本条除非在国会将其提交各州之日起七年以内，由四分之三州议会批准为宪法修正案，不得发生效力。

第二十三条修正案
［1960 年 6 月 16 日提出，1961 年 3 月 29 日批准］

第一款　合众国政府所在的特区，应依国会规定方式选派：一定数目的总统和副总统选举人，其人数如同特区是一个州一样，等于它在国会有权拥有的参议员和众议员人数的总和，但不得超过人口最少之州的选举人人数。他们是在各州所选派的举人以外增添的人，但为了选举总统和副总统的目的，应被视为一个州选派的选举人；他们在特区集会，履行第十二条修正案所规定的职责。

第二款　国会有权以适当立法实施本条。

第二十四条修正案
［1962 年 8 月 27 日提出，1964 年 1 月 23 日批准］

第一款　合众国公民在总统或副总统、总统或副总统选举人、或国会参议员或众议员的任何预选或其他选举中的选举权，不得因未交纳任何人头税或其他税而被合众国或任何一州加以拒绝或限制。

第二款　国会有权以适当立法实施本条。

第二十五条修正案
［1965 年 7 月 6 日提出，1967 年 2 月 10 日批准］

Section 1   In case of the removal of the President from office or of his death or resignation, the Vice President shall become President.

Section 2   Whenever there is a vacancy in the office of the Vice President, the President shall nominate a Vice President who shall take office upon confirmation by a majority vote of both Houses of Congress.

Section 3   Whenever the President transmits to the President pro tempore of the Senate and the Speaker of the House of Representatives his written declaration that he is unable to discharge the powers and duties of his office, and until he transmits to them a written declaration to the contrary, such powers and duties shall be discharged by the Vice President as Acting President.

Section 4   Whenever the Vice President and a majority of either the principal officers of the executive departments or of such other body as Congress may by law provide, transmit to the President pro tempore of the Senate and the Speaker of the House of Representatives their written declaration that the President is unable to discharge the powers and duties of his office, the Vice President shall immediately assume the powers and duties of the office as Acting President.

Thereafter, when the President transmits to the President pro tempore of the Senate and the Speaker of the House of Representatives his written declaration that no inability exists, he shall resume the powers and duties of his office unless the Vice President and a majority of either the principal officers of the executive department or of such other body as Congress may by law provide, transmit within four days to the President pro tempore of the Senate and the Speaker of the House of Representatives their written declaration that the President is unable to discharge the powers and duties of his office. Thereupon Congress shall decide the issue, assembling within forty-eight hours for that purpose if not in session. If the Congress, within twenty-one days after receipt of the latter written declaration, or, if Congress is not in session, within twenty-one days after Congress is required to assemble, determines by two-thirds vote of both Houses that the President is unable to discharge the powers and duties of his office, the Vice President shall continue to discharge the same as Acting President; otherwise, the President shall resume the powers and duties of his office.

第一款　如遇总统被免职、死亡或辞职，副总统应成为总统。

第二款　凡当副总统职位出缺时，总统应提名一名副总统，经国会两院都以过半数票批准后就职。

第三款　凡当总统向参议院临时议长和众议院议长提交书面声明，声称他不能够履行其职务的权力和责任，直至他向他们提交一份相反的声明为止，其权力和责任应由副总统作为代理总统履行。

第四款　凡当副总统和行政各部长官的多数或国会以法律设立的其他机构成员的多数，向参议院临时议长和众议院议长提交书面声明，声称总统不能够履行总统职务的权力和责任时，副总统应立即作为代理总统承担总统职务的权力和责任。

此后，当总统向参议院临时议长和众议院议长提交书面声明，声称丧失能力的情况不存在时，他应恢复总统职务的权力和责任，除非副总统和行政各部长官的多数或国会以法律设立的其它机构成员的多数在四天之内向参议院临时议长和众议院议长提交书面声明，声称总统不能够履行总统职务的权力和责任。在此种情况下，国会应决定这一问题，如在休会期间，应为此目的在四十八小时以内集会。如国会在收到后一书面声明后的二十一天以内，或如适逢休会期间，则在国会按照要求集会以后的二十一天以内，以两院的三分之二的票数决定总统不能够履行总统职务的权力和责任，副总统应继续作为代理总统履行总统职务的权力和责任；否则总统应恢复总统职务的权力和责任。

AMENDMENT XXVI

Passed by Congress March 23, 1971. Ratified July 1, 1971.

Note: Amendment 14, section 2, of the Constitution was modified by section 1 of the 26th amendment.

Section 1   The right of citizens of the United States, who are eighteen years of age or older, to vote shall not be denied or abridged by the United States or by any State on account of age.

Section 2   The Congress shall have power to enforce this article by appropriate legislation.

AMENDMENT XXVII

Originally proposed Sept. 25, 1789. Ratified May 7, 1992.

No law, varying the compensation for the services of the Senators and Representatives, shall take effect, until an election of representatives shall have intervened.

第二十六条修正案

［1971 年 3 月 23 日提出，1971 年 7 月 1 日批准］

第一款　年满十八岁和十八岁以上的合众国公民的选举权，不得因为年龄而被合众国或任何一州加以拒绝或限制。

第二款　国会有权以适当立法实施本条。

第二十七条修正案

［1989 年 9 月 25 日提出，1992 年 5 月 7 日批准］

改变参议员和众议员服务报酬的法律，在众议员选举举行之前不得生效。

（本译本引用自李道揆《美国政府和美国政治》，商务印书馆，1999-03 版）

FOUNDATIONS of DEMOCRACY